D1623028

Retrospective Conversion
A PRACTICAL
GUIDE FOR LIBRARIES

Supplements to
Computers in Libraries

Retrospective Conversion
A PRACTICAL
GUIDE FOR LIBRARIES

Jane Beaumont
and
Joseph P. Cox

Meckler
Westport • London

Library of Congress Cataloging-in-Publication Data

Beaumont, Jane, 1945-
    Retrospective conversion : a practical guide for libraries /
by Jane Beaumont and Joseph P. Cox.
        p. cm. -- (Supplements to computers in libraries ; 7)
        Bibliography : p.
        Includes index.
        ISBN 0-88736-352-0 (alk. paper) : $
        1. Retrospective conversion (Cataloging) 2. Recataloging -- Data
processing. 3. Catalogs, On-line. 4. Microcomputers -- Library
applications. 5. Small libraries--Automation.   I. Cox, Joseph P.
II. Title.   III. Series.
Z699. 35 . R48B43   1989
025.3 ' 028 ' 5--dc19   88-13389
                                                                  CIP

British Cataloguing in Publication Data

Beaumont, Jane, *1945-*
    Retrospective conversion : a practical
    guide for libraries.
    1. Libraries. Applications of microcomputer systems
    I. Title II. Cox, Joseph P.
    025 ' .0028 ' 5416

    ISBN 0-88736-352-0

Meckler Corporation, 11 Ferry Lane West, Westport, CT 06880.
Meckler Ltd., Grosvenor Gardens House, Grosvenor Gardens,
    London SW1W 0BS, U.K.

Printed on acid free paper.
Printed in the United States of America.

Table of Contents

Acknowledgments

This volume would not have been completed without the encouragement of those who attended Joe Cox's workshops on retrospective conversion and Jane Beaumont's clients. We would like to thank them for their interest and constructive comments. We would also like to acknowledge and thank the following experts who reviewed our draft manuscript and made many useful suggestions: Elizabeth Black, Utlas International; Mike Campbell, City of York Board of Eduction; C. Donald Cook, Faculty of Library and Information Science, University of Toronto; and Ingrid Parent, National Library of Canada. While we have incorporated many of their suggestions and corrections, any remaining errors are solely our responsibility.

Acronyms and Abbreviations

AACR2	*Anglo-American Cataloguing Rules, Second Edition*
ANSI	American National Standards Institute
BSI	British Standards Institution
CANMARC	Canadian MARC
CD-ROM	Compact disc-read only memory
CSA	Canadian Standards Association
CSH	*Canadian Subject Headings*
DDC	*Dewey Decimal Classification*
ISBD	International Standard Bibliographic Description
ISBN	International Standard Book Number
ISO	International Organization for Standardization
LC	Library of Congress
LCC	*Library of Congress Classification*
LCCN	Library of Congress Card Number
LCSH	*Library of Congress Subject Headings*
MARC	MAchine Readable Cataloging
MESH	*Medical Subject Headings*
NISO	National Information Standards Organization
NLC	National Library of Canada
OCR	Optical character recognition
UKMARC	United Kingdom MARC
USMARC	United States MARC

Introduction

The purpose of this book is to provide information in nontechnical language about converting a card catalog to machine-readable format for use with an automated library system. This process is now well known as recon, meaning retrospective conversion. In fact the word 'recon' is so well established in our lives as practicing librarians that we have chosen to treat it as a word rather than an acronym. It is our intention to provide the essential information for organizing a recon project, creating or obtaining appropriate machine-readable records, and establishing ongoing procedures for online cataloging.

Until recently it was difficult for librarians in small- and medium-sized libraries to justify the expense of automation but now the cost of equipment is coming down and good library packages are available for microcomputers. As a result, librarians with little or no experience in library automation are obtaining automated library systems and are faced with the prospect of converting a card catalog to machine-readable format and sometimes becoming conversant with the use of MARC fields and online cataloging practices. It is these librarians who are the intended audience of this book; however, anyone contemplating a recon project will undoubtedly find many useful tips in the following chapters.

Retrospective Conversion: A Practical Guide for Libraries provides information in the following chapters:

Chapter 1. What is Retrospective Conversion and Why Do It? This chapter explains what recon is, answers the question 'Why do it?', and explains why some libraries choose not to do recon.

Chapter 2. The Recon Process: An Overview. This chapter introduces the reader to the recon process and provides an overview of how to do a recon project.

Chapters 3-5. Planning for a Recon Project. In this section the authors set the scene for recon and the preparatory steps that need to be taken. The chapters contain discussions of the methods for determining the library's needs, outline the process of establishing parameters and standards for the project, and describe crucial decisions that have to be made during the planning process.

Chapters 6–8. Identifying and Choosing a Recon Option. These chapters outline the various options for doing recon, including doing it in-house or sending it out to a commercial vendor. The advantages and disadvantages of each option are discussed.

In conjunction with this chapter, Appendix I, Sources of MARC Records and Recon Services, contains a selected list of recon agencies available in the United States and Canada. The authors analyse the options in terms of library resources, existing catalogs, and requirements. Vendors and cost components are considered in preparation for determining the total cost of the project and choosing a recon option.

Chapter 9. Develop an Action Plan for the Recon Project. Having decided on the approach to recon, the final decisions and steps that need to be made before implementing the project are discussed.

Chapter 10. MAchine-Readable Cataloging (MARC). This chapter explains what MARC is, and the importance of MARC in automated library systems and resource sharing. The elements of MARC—formats, fixed and variable fields, subfields and indicators—are also described.

Chapters 11–12. MARC Bibliographic and Authority Records. These chapters provide field-by-field guides to various segments of MARC bibliographic and authority records. It is intended that the reader should use these chapters as a guide to the level of coding appropriate to small- and medium-sized libraries and as a manual for ongoing coding practices. Authority control and the relationship of authority records to bibliographic records are described. The components of a MARC authority record are discussed, and the principles and importance of having authority control are evaluated.

Chapter 13. Implementation and Project Management. This chapter guides the reader through the process of selecting appropriate coding levels for small- and medium-sized libraries. Each field is described and examples are given to relate the catalog card information to a MARC record. The options for describing local holdings fields are given, and guidelines are provided for developing a suitable profile of fields for the automated system. The implementation of MARC in a library is discussed in terms of standards and procedures to follow in loading recon records and ongoing cataloging.

Chapter 14. Editing Derived Records. The decisions that have to be made regarding editing records derived from an external source are described, and the reader is guided in developing a plan of action, assigning resources, and preparing procedures.

The final comments in the manual are intended to bring together the approaches to recon that are discussed in preceding chapters and to re-emphasize the importance of determining needs before commencing such a project.

We have also included four appendices: a comparative chart of recon services; a directory of firms and organizations providing MARC records and recon services; sample worksheets; and a selected bibliography.

Throughout this book the authors use a number of terms that may be new to librarians learning about automation, so these are defined below:

Application software: The collective name for computer programs that apply the computer to the user's required tasks. For example, library collection control, word processing, and accounting programs.

Database: In library automation terms it is the machine-readable equivalent of the card catalog. Each unique title is represented once in the database and access to the information is through the indexes that are built and managed by the application software. In some ways the indexes are analogous to the index of a book but instead of page numbers associated with authors, subjects, etc., the computer stores pointers to where that information is located on the computer storage medium. The library application software manages this database and displays information in response to user requests.

File: A group of records for one type of information stored in the database. For example, a library database may contain separate files for bibliographic descriptions, serials check-in information, vendor names and addresses, on-order information, patron information, etc. These files are linked through common pieces of information and are manipulated by the applications programs.

Hit rate: The percentage of titles from the library's shelf-list that match records in a vendor's database and can be derived (copied) for use in the library's machine-readable database. For example, if a library found matches for 850 records out of 1,000 searched, the hit rate would be 85 percent.

Record: Each unique entity in a file is represented by a record. In a bibliographic file each unique title and/or edition requires a separate record. In the patron file each person is represented by a record.

Fields and subfields: The record is subdivided into fields. Each field contains unique information that describes an attribute or characteristic of the item represented by the record. For example, author, title, imprint, and subject description are each stored in different fields of a bibliographic record. Each field has a label (or tag) that is used to tell the library application software what kind of information the field contains. MARC fields are further subdivided into subfields which are labelled with delimiters, again to indicate to the application program the special characteristics of the information.

In this manual we are primarily concerned with the creation of machine-readable bibliographic records. In an automated system one bibliographic record will represent each unique title in the library collection. 'Uniqueness' will be decided in much the same way as it was in the manual environment and is the machine equivalent of an individual card set in the catalog. It may be a combination of unique title, edition, place, publisher, and date. The cataloging policies which the library has established in the manual environment may be continued in the automated environment. The machine-readable bibliographic record created through the recon project will contain:

- the bibliographic description, equivalent to the description on the old unit card in the catalog
- codes defined in the MARC standard for the communication of machine-readable bibliographic records
- details of the library's own holdings, including the call number and location of each copy or volume associated with the title. This information is equivalent to the notes that are often pencilled on the back of the shelf-list card in a manual catalog.
- access points such as authors, editors, illustrators, titles and uniform titles, and series
- subject headings to provide access to the subject content of the work

We hope that you will be able to use this book as a guide from the start to finish of the recon project and as an ongoing manual on the use of MARC coding for online cataloging. The primary audience for the book is librarians in small- and medium-sized libraries of all types. However, our experience with larger libraries indicates that many of the techniques and details discussed will also be of interest to this audience.

At the end of each chapter we have provided references to further reading on the topic of that chapter. A complete bibliography of the references is included in Appendix IV. We have also closed each chapter with a summary of the topics covered in the chapter, which we hope can be used as a checklist to the steps involved in planning and implementing a recon project and introducing MARC coding to your library.

Our hope is that describing the steps in detail will remove some of the mystique of library automation and show that with an understanding of your automation needs, careful planning, and adequate resources, you too can replace the card catalog with a machine-readable database and enter the community of automated libraries.

1
What is Retrospective Conversion
and Why Do It?

Retrospective conversion (recon) is a costly and time-consuming undertaking for most libraries. Frequently, it has to be fitted in as a special project, competing with the day to day activities of the library. For the person who has to plan and execute the project, the preparations are time-consuming and the decisions along the way are numerous. The objective of this handbook is to provide a guide to the preparatory work, to outline the decisions to be made, and to provide practical guidelines on how to execute a recon project. Thus we want to assist libraries in carrying out an efficient, cost-effective, and quality project. In this chapter, we are going to define recon, give various reasons for undertaking a project, and also look at some of the objections to recon.

What is Retrospective Conversion?

Retrospective conversion is the conversion of a library's existing bibliographic records from manual to machine-readable format according to specified policies and standards.

From the definition it is clear that recon is concerned not with ongoing cataloging, but rather with converting previously created bibliographic records from card or paper format to machine-readable format. Recon is not cataloging or even recataloging (although sometimes the latter may be necessary or useful to make changes to older headings, classification numbers, etc.). A library must be careful not to overestimate what it will accomplish with the project. The primary purpose is to create a machine-readable file of the existing manual catalog, not to duplicate the labors of previous catalogers. Recon is the conversion of data from one format to another, as quickly and as inexpensively as possible, while maintaining the policies and standards set for the project. Many policy decisions must be made before the project is begun, such as: how much editing is to be done?; are all names to be checked in an authority file?, etc. Standards for the project have also to be decided upon, such as: will the *Anglo-American Cataloguing Rules, Second Edition* (*AACR2*) be followed faithfully?; is the machine-readable cataloging (MARC) format to be used?, etc. Setting standards for the project is, perhaps, one of the most troublesome aspects of a recon project, and one which this handbook will deal with at length. At various points in the text we will also indicate when it is necessary to decide upon and record policy decisions. It is enough to say at this stage that for a project to be successfully accomplished, certain policies and standards must be decided upon before the project begins and they must be adhered to during its execution.

By the time you have read through this handbook and chosen some of the options available, the scope and complexity of the project that you wish to undertake should be clear to you. The conversion of the catalog must be tailor-made to suit the particular situation and needs of your library, while keeping in mind the above definition of recon.

Why Are You Doing Recon?

The reasons for undertaking a recon project are many and varied, and reflect the particular needs of your library. We can divide the reasons into two main groups: local considerations and regional, national, and international considerations.

Local Considerations

To create a database for a local automation system. This can be cited as the primary reason for wishing to undertake a recon project. The library usually wishes to automate the circulation function in the library and/or to provide an online catalog. The library may also wish to provide for its future automation needs and in fact proceeds to carry out a recon project without having a specific automation system in place. The need to have a machine-readable file of its bibliographic records has, however, been identified.

To improve service to users. If a library is to undertake a costly project such as recon, it should be sure that certain benefits accrue from the project. It is to be expected that the results improve the services that the library provides its users. Some of the benefits which library users may find are improved circulation services, improved access to the library's collections, improved interlibrary loan response time, etc.

To improve internal library procedures. Not only should a library expect that a recon project will benefit its users, it should also expect that the project will assist the library's own staff in accomplishing their tasks with more efficiency. This may manifest itself in such benefits as the elimination of card filing, the availability of more current bibliographic data, the lessening of time-consuming changes to catalog records, and an improvement in pre-order and pre-cataloging searching.

To generate special products. If a library has its catalog in machine-readable format, it is much easier to generate special products, including a complete database produced in a different format (e.g., a microfiche catalog to be distributed at various points in the library or to different branches) or a subset of the database, (e.g., a serials catalog, or a catalog of the library's 16mm films). Once the data have been entered into the library's database in a consistent format, with useful coding, it is possible to generate many special products. The library's catalog is no longer site-bound and can be accessed more easily.

To create an integrated file and to eliminate the cost of maintaining parallel systems. One of the reasons many libraries contemplate a recon project is that present cataloging is automated while older records remain in card format. This creates two files and hence two places to search for library materials. It is quite common for a library to have some of its records on microfiche or in an online catalog, and the remainder in a card catalog. This is awkward for both users and library staff. With a complete recon, the library acquires a single, integrated file. The cost of maintaining two catalogs has also become prohibitive for some libraries and they simply close the card catalog and maintain just one catalog. Other libraries maintain both catalogs. Neither solution is very satisfactory. When the recon project is completed, however, the need to maintain parallel catalogs is eliminated and hence catalog maintenance costs are reduced.

To provide flexibility in changing systems. It is evident that the rate of technological change is very rapid. Some of the libraries who were the first to automate have now changed systems two or three times. A library must therefore try to create a database which will allow it to move with technological change. Having an integrated machine-readable file will allow libraries to move from older to newer computer systems with more ease and less cost.

To maximize return on automation expenditures. Libraries are spending vast amounts of money on computer hardware and software. If, for instance, only fifty percent of a library's catalog is in the automated system then the library is not maximizing the return on its investment. Besides not using its computer power to full potential, the library is probably wasting time and money using and maintaining two systems, a manual one and an automated one.

To protect library files. One of the attributes of machine-readable catalogs is their portability, as opposed to card catalogs, which are usually maintained at a single site. This portability provides added protection to the library's bibliographic files as copies of the files can be stored and maintained in off-site locations. In the event of flood, fire, or other disasters in the library, the file copies remain safe. Preservation of the files should not pose a problem in the future as they can be copied and transferred to newer and better means of storage as these become available.

Regional, National, and International Considerations

To create union lists. For libraries which are part of a larger library system or group of libraries, having all the holdings in machine-readable format can facilitate the production of union lists, which can be a cumbersome task if maintained manually.

To share bibliographic data. The conversion of a library's bibliographic records to machine-readable format means that the data can be shared with other libraries. This is especially true for those libraries which form a consortium or maintain files with bibliographic utilities. This sharing of data is of mutual value to the member libraries as the pool of available records increases.

To share bibliographic resources. Not only is the bibliographic data made more widely available when in machine-readable format, the bibliographic items themselves are often more widely available to other libraries. Through the use of central databases and electronic mail the interlibrary loan function in many libraries, especially smaller ones, has been greatly enhanced by the ability to identify a location for an item, and subsequently to make an interlibrary loan request for it.

To facilitate collection rationalization. The decision whether or not to purchase a specific item can be aided if the library in question has access to all bibliographic records of similar neighboring libraries. With automated union catalogs and bibliographic consortia, it is easy to explore the holdings of other libraries.

To create national databases and to contribute to universal bibliographic control. Having the library's records in machine-readable format can extend the benefits beyond the local and regional arenas to the national and international. When libraries contribute cataloging to a larger pool they are increasing the number of records available to all who use that pool. They are aiding the bibliographic control of items in their own area and contribute to universal bibliographic control.

Why Would You Not Do Recon?

Many of the reasons for doing recon as stated above have always been a part of librarianship and can be achieved in a manual system as well as in an automated one. For this and other reasons, some libraries have decided that the conversion of their catalogs is not a priority, and is, in fact, sometimes unnecessary. Some of the reasons why libraries decide not to convert all their holdings are as follows.

Too costly. The conversion of bibliographic records to machine-readable format is rarely inexpensive and the competing demands on library budgets place recon outside some libraries' immediate spending priorities.

Only a core collection need be in machine-readable format. Practically every library has a segment of its collection which is heavily used, while other areas of the collection are rarely used or borrowed. While the decision to convert depends on the type of library and the needs of its users (for example, research versus public), some librarians choose not to convert those segments of the collection that are not frequently used.

Unnecessary to convert older materials. The decision is also sometimes made not to convert the older materials in one's collection, because librarians surmise, or demonstrate, that older materials are not used as much as newer materials. Again, this can depend on the type of library and users. It can sometimes be demonstrated that a high proportion of requests for materials can be satisfied from a small proportion of the collection and that many of the requests are satisfied with more recent acquisitions. Hence the decision not to convert the bibliographic records for those older materials.

Bibliographic records are available in another format. The argument can be made that if a librarian decides not to convert all the library's holdings to machine-readable format, the library user is not left high and dry. There still remains a source of access to these records, usually the card catalog.

Before finally deciding whether to do a recon project or not, it may be useful to read the following chapter and learn a bit more about the recon process.

Checklist:
What is Retrospective Conversion and Why Do It?

Definition

Retrospective conversion is the conversion of a library's existing bibliographic records from manual to machine-readable format according to specified policies and standards.

Why Are You Doing Recon?

Local Considerations

- to create a database for a local automation system
- to improve service to users
- to improve internal library procedures
- to generate special products
- to create an integrated file and eliminate the cost of maintaining parallel systems
- to provide flexibility in switching systems
- to maximize the return on automation expenditures
- to protect library files

Regional, National, and International Considerations

- to create union lists
- to share bibliographic data
- to share bibliographic resources
- to facilitate collection rationalization
- to create national databases and to facilitate universal bibliographic control

Why Would You Not Do Recon?

- too costly
- only a core collection need be in machine-readable format
- unnecessary to convert older materials
- bibliographic records are available in another format

Further Reading

Awcock, Frances. "Retrospective Conversion: Pipedream or Practicality?" *Australian Library Journal* 34 (February 1985): 11-18.

Boss, Richard. "Retrospective Conversion: Investing in the Future." *Wilson Library Bulletin* 59 (November 1984): 173-78.

Burger, Robert H. "Conversion of Catalog Records to Machine-Readable Form: Major Projects, Continuing Problems, and Future Prospects." *Cataloging & Classification Quarterly* 3 (Fall 1982): 27-40.

Dwyer, James R. "The Effect of Closed Catalogs on Public Access." *Library Resources & Technical Services* 25 (April-June 1981): 186-95.

Hirshon, Arnold. "The Emperor's Bibliographic Clothes." *RTSD Newsletter* 10, no. 3 (1985): 28-30.

Hoare, Peter A. "Retrospective Catalogue Conversion in British University Libraries: A Survey and a Discussion of Problems." *British Journal of Academic Librarianship* 1 (Summer 1986): 95-131.

Jones, C. Lee. "Issues in Retrospective Conversion." *College & Research Libraries News* 45 (November 1984): 528-32.

Matthews, Joseph R., Joan Frye Williams. "Oh, If I'd Only Known: Ten Things You Can Do Today to Prepare for Library Automation Tomorrow." *American Libraries* 14 (June 1983): 408-12.

Petersen, Karla D. "Planning for Serials Retrospective Conversion." *Serials Review* 10 (Fall 1984): 73-8.

Racine, Drew. "Retrospective Conversion: A Challenge (Still) Facing Academic Libraries." *Show-Me Libraries* 36 (October-November 1984): 39-43.

2
The Recon Process: An Overview

This chapter provides an overview of the recon process, which will be discussed in detail in the next seven chapters. At first sight, the process of developing a recon project may seem rather onerous. For the project to be successful—that is, to be both cost-effective and efficient—forethought and planning are essential. It is necessary for a library to know clearly what it wants to achieve with the project, the options available for carrying it out, the cost implications of each option, and the most efficient way for proceeding with the selected option. In the following chapters consideration will be given to the eight areas of concern as set out below.

The Recon Process

Determine library needs. It is imperative for a library to determine its automation and machine-readable data needs. In this context, we will look at both present and future needs. With regard to present needs, the immediate goal of recon must be established, the automated cataloging methods already in place, if any, must be examined, and the overall automation situation of the library must be taken into account. With regard to future needs, the medium- and long-term plans for automation should be considered to determine the impact of such plans on the scope, standards, and quality of the recon project.

Establish parameters for the recon project. Before meaningful parameters can be set for a project, it is necessary to know the content of the library's collection and how it is used. This includes knowing the overall extent of the collection, the subject and form divisions within that collection, and in general terms the use made of the various parts of the collection. This information is especially vital if only a portion of the collection can be converted at one time. Once this information is known, one, some or all of the following parameters can be used to limit the scope of the project:

- circulation or use
- date range
- classification range
- time frame

- cost ceilings
- reclassification
- recataloging

Establish standards for the recon project. Some of the most crucial decisions to be made in planning the recon project are in the area of standards. To establish standards for the recon project is to determine the level of acceptance by an individual library of generally accepted and widely used cataloging codes and machine-readable record format structures. While standards may be established by an agency outside a library, they are usually accepted or modified by the individual library and are determined by library needs. We must consider, therefore, how standards and library needs, both present and future, are dependent upon one another. While standards depend on needs, they also have a great impact on the cost of a recon project. Therefore, the cost implications of local acceptance of certain standards must be considered. It is necessary in this discussion to examine the following standards:

- level of fullness of the cataloging record
- the use of AACR2
- the use of the MARC format
- the use of subject access systems
- the use of classification systems
- the use of authority control devices

Identify recon options. The options available to libraries for recon are many and varied. Each one has advantages and disadvantages and the library must consider its options carefully. We will identify options and consider the implications of recon carried out:

- in-house
- by an outside recon vendor
- a combination of in-house and vendor recon

Appendix I contains detailed information on various vendors of recon services and provides practical examples of this more theoretical discussion.

Analyze options. Once a library has identified some potential options for recon, it is necessary to examine those options in more detail. This will allow the library to explore the impact of each option on library resources, and to identify the qualities and characteristics of specific options. When analyzing options a library will consider:

- library resources
- library catalogs
- library requirements
- vendor characteristics
- vendor requirements

In the analysis of options it is obviously essential to look at costs. For each option chosen for analysis it is necessary to determine the costs for the following:

- staff
- equipment and supplies
- vendor or utility charges

Determining costs has proven difficult for many libraries involved in a recon project as there are so many variables at work, and not all are fully known prior to the commencement of the project. For this reason, in Chapter 7 there is a lengthy discussion of how to identify the variables for each option, and how to establish common characteristics by which costs can be compared.

Choose an option. Having gathered the necessary data as outlined above, a library is now in a position to decide which option to choose. The ideal situation would be to find the option which offers the lowest cost, the highest quality, and the one with least negative impact on the library. However, what is likely to be chosen is a compromise between cost, quality, and impact.

Develop plan of action. After choosing a method of recon, it is time to get down to the details of how to carry out the project. Whether it is to be carried out in-house, by an outside vendor, or through a combination of the two, it is necessary to assign supervisory staff to the project, specifically someone who will be directly responsible for its execution. Following this, it is necessary to establish written policies for the project, detailed enough to allow recon staff to proceed in a consistent manner. Chapter 14 deals with policy issues, especially in the area of editing of records acquired from an outside source. As well as written policies, detailed user manuals should be provided for staff, particularly if the staff are newly recruited for the project and are unfamiliar with library policies and procedures. Developing the plan of action also involves determining staffing requirements and initiating the recruitment process. Finally comes the task of allocating the necessary resources for the project, including staff, equipment and supplies, work location, and money.

Implement the project, monitor progress, fine tune procedures, and complete the project. While the project is being carried out it is likely that changes will have to be made to certain procedures. Flexibility should be allowed for in policies and procedures in order to advance the project to its ultimate conclusion.

This chapter was intended to provide an overview of the recon process. We are now going to look at each step in much greater detail.

Checklist:
The Recon Process: An Overview

- determine library needs
- establish parameters for the recon project
- establish standards for the recon project
- identify recon options
- analyze options
- choose an option
- develop a plan of action
- implement the project, fine tune procedures, complete the project

Further Reading

Asher, Richard E. "Retrospective Conversion of Bibliographic Records." *Catholic Library World* 54 (November 1982): 155-61.

Boss, Richard. "Retrospective Conversion: Investing in the Future." *Wilson Library Bulletin* 59 (November 1984): 173-78.

Butler, Brett, Brian Aveney, and William Scholz. "The Conversion of Manual Catalogs to Collection Data Bases." *Library Technology Reports* 14 (March-April 1978): 109-206.

Carter, Ruth C., and Scott Bruntjen. *Data Conversion.* Professional Librarian Series. White Plains, NY: Knowledge Industry Publications, 1983.

Gorman, Michael. "The Economics of Catalog Conversion." In *Proceedings of the 1976 Clinic on Library Applications of Data Processing: The Economics of Library Automation*, edited by J.L. Divilbiss. Champaign, IL: University of Illinois, Graduate School of Library Science, 1977.

McQueen, Judy, and Richard W. Boss. "Sources of Machine-Readable Cataloging and Retrospective Conversion." *Library Technology Reports* 21 (November-December 1985): 601-732.

Reed-Scott, Jutta, Dorothy Gregor, and Charles Payne. *Issues in Retrospective Conversion: Report of a Study Conducted for the Council on Library Resources.* Washington, DC: Council on Library Resources, 1984.

3
Determining Library Needs

The objective of the recon project is to create or to acquire cataloging records in machine-readable format. Before commencing a recon project it is imperative for a library to determine its machine-readable data needs. For this reason, let us look at the issues involved in both present and future needs.

Present Needs

Immediate goal of recon. The library should know what is to be achieved by the recon project. Usually recon is in preparation for the automation of a specific function in the library. Many libraries begin a recon project because they have the opportunity to implement an automated circulation system and need collection information in machine-readable format to support it. Other libraries need the records for a forthcoming online catalog. If, for instance, the library intends to implement a circulation system, it may well be the case that only a portion of the manual records need to be converted initially, given that not all items circulate simultaneously. If, however, an online catalog is to be developed, it may be necessary to have proportionally more manual records converted as the online catalog is to be the locating device for library materials. For libraries which already have automation systems in place, the objective of the recon project is often to create a complete, machine-readable file of the library's holdings. Clearly a need for recon must be demonstrated before the project gets under way.

Automated cataloging methods in place. It is necessary to see how the present automated cataloging situation would tie in with the recon methodology chosen and the resulting machine-readable records. If, for instance, a library is using a bibliographic utility for ongoing cataloging, it must determine that the format of the converted records is compatible with that of its current cataloging records. Many in-house systems accept records from numerous sources and reformat the records to suit the system. It is necessary to make sure that any converted data is suitable for use with the present system, or compatible with records derived from that system. If a library follows national and international standards in its cataloging activity and in the conversion of the catalog, there should be few complications. When purchasing cataloging data from any source, the library must inquire as to its structure and portability.

Overall automation situation. The recon project must be placed in the context of the overall automation situation. If a number of functions in the library are automated, such as acquisitions, cataloging, interlibrary loans, or production of union catalogs, and they are presently supported by ongoing cataloging data, then the end product of the recon project should also be able to support them. The quality and completeness of the converted records must also be considered. If, for instance, a library's online catalog provides sophisticated Boolean searching, then the converted records must have the coding and data necessary to take advantage of this facility.

Future Needs

What are the medium- and long-term plans for automation? These are never easy questions to answer, especially considering the pace of technological change. It is important at this stage to provide the library of the future with as much leeway as possible to deal with change as it arises. The data you convert or the system you convert to should not restrict the library in its future automation developments. If a library expects to provide advanced searching techniques in the future, then it should produce the data now that will allow this to occur. If you intend to retire outdated computer hardware and software in the near future, then you must make sure that data converted now can be used on newer systems.

In effect, it is necessary to establish the current, near future, and long-term applications and goals of the library's machine-readable records, and automation in general. In this way the library will be able to establish two essential aspects of the recon project: parameters and standards. The next two chapters describe these characteristics in detail.

Checklist:
Determining Library Needs

- Present needs

    - immediate goal of recon
    - automated cataloging methods in place
    - overall automation situation

- Future needs

    - medium- and long-term automation plans

- Needs have an impact on

    - parameters of the recon project
    - standards of the recon project

Further Reading

Carter, Ruth C., and Scott Bruntjen. *Data Conversion.* Professional Librarian Series. White Plains, N.Y.: Knowledge Industry Publications, 1983.

"Loading Separate Bibliographic Files on an Automated System." *Library Systems Newsletter* 4 (September 1984): 69-71.

4
Establishing Parameters for the Recon Project

It is unusual for a library to have the resources to convert its entire catalog to machine-readable format at one time. It is therefore necessary decide which parts of the collection will be converted and in which sequence. To establish parameters is to decide on the size and scope of the recon project. If you have first of all determined what your immediate recon needs are—for example, records for the circulation system—then you can use a combination of the factors as set out below to determine which parts of the collection need to be converted.

Establishing Parameters

Identify Collection Content

It is necessary to know one's library collection. This is easier said than done. The taking of inventory and detailed weeding are infrequent events in some libraries. In fact, it is advisable to do both of these tasks before the recon project is begun. While the two tasks have obvious benefits in their own right for the library and its users, they will also contribute to a more efficient and less costly recon project. You do not have time or resources to create records for titles which, in effect, do not or should not exist in the library.

While precision in identifying the collection is not essential, try to have good estimates in terms of size and scope. If a shelf-list exists it is possible to determine, for instance, how many catalog records take up an inch of space in a shelf-list drawer, determine how many inches of shelf-list there are, and then multiply that number by the number of records per inch. (It is useful to determine an average number of records per inch by sampling a number of drawers first). If no shelf-list exists it will be obviously more difficult to determine the size of the collection (and more difficult to do the recon project too!), unless the collection is small. In any case, knowledge of the collection and its size is essential and the library must devise a method of acquiring the information required.

Practical Parameters

Some libraries have used the following methods or combinations of them to set the parameters of the recon project.

Circulation or use. Circulation statistics and/or general staff awareness can be called on to determine the parts of the collection or the items in the collection which are the most heavily used. This is intended to identify the areas of the collection which should be converted first.

Date range. From the above circulation information it may also be possible to determine the date of publication of the items circulated. For example, it may become clear that 85 percent of all borrowing is for books published after 1975. Therefore, if everything published after 1975 is converted, it may be possible to satisfy 85 percent of library users' requests. Naturally it depends on the type of library and the type of library users. Some libraries decide on a date range and subsequently tell their users that everything published after, for instance, 1975 is in the online catalog, while materials published before 1975 can be located in the card catalog. If a library is considering using a date range as a cutoff point for recon it should also keep in mind the method chosen to obtain the machine-readable records. It is necessary to know the date range of the database from which the records are being extracted. For instance, the LC MARC database contains records created since 1968, so to convert all records from 1960 using Library of Congress records, it may be necessary to select an additional vendor or locate the records elsewhere.

Classification range. Another method that can be used to limit the size of the recon project is to convert whole classification sections of the collection rather than parts of all sections. In this case you would identify the most important sections of the collection to be converted first. For some libraries it could be the 900s in Dewey, or the P schedules in LC. Again it depends upon the type of library, its collections and its users.

Time frame. As well as establishing parameters for the parts of the collection to be converted, it is also advisable for the smooth running of the project to work within a certain time frame. Needless to say, this is difficult to determine as it is not possible to know beforehand all the variables which are involved in a recon project, such as hit rate, amount of editing, if any, to be done to retrieved records, etc. However, for both budgeting purposes and for staff morale, it is beneficial to put time limits on the project. Recon projects have a way of developing a life of their own and can drag on indefinitely, leading to loss of output and of morale. Set time frames as goals to be achieved and try to produce as much as possible in the time allocated.

Cost ceilings. Establishing a cost ceiling is perhaps even more important to the success of the recon project than establishing a time frame. Again it is always difficult to predict how much a recon project will cost, but after reading this handbook you will be able to identify cost components and accurately estimate the budget. The advantage of having a cost ceiling is that it is easy to spend money on recon and to expand the project as time goes on without intentionally doing so. It is useful to have a mechanism in place which will indicate when too much money is being spent per record.

Reclassification. Some libraries use recon as an opportunity to reclassify parts of their collection. This can be a good time for such an operation, especially if a library is obtaining records which provide classification numbers of the scheme it intends to use. Reclassifying part of a collection will add to the cost of the project as each book in question must be retrieved, a cutter or book number applied to the classification number, and new label and pocket prepared and applied to the book. Then the book has to be re-shelved. All these costs must be built into the cost estimate for the project and known in advance.

Recataloging. Recataloging is a thorny issue in a recon project. If we revert to our definition of recon we said it is the conversion of existing bibliographic records. If one undertakes to recatalog the collection the project will probably never be completed! One must be prepared to trust the cataloging of previous catalogers and live with less than perfect records according to presently accepted standards, such as *AACR2*, current *Library of Congress Subject Headings (LCSH)* practice, etc. Before the project begins certain policies regarding recataloging must be formulated and they must be clear to recon staff members. A more thorough discussion of standards and editing of records will appear in Chapter 5 and Chapter 14 respectively. These will help you to formulate such policies.

Checklist:
Establishing Parameters for the Recon Project

Parameters

To establish parameters is to decide on the size and scope of the recon project.

Practical Parameters

- circulation or use
- date range
- classification range
- time frame
- cost ceilings
- reclassification
- recataloging

Further Reading

Information Systems Consultants Inc. *Retrospective Conversion for the Libraries of McGill University.* N.p.: Information Systems Consultants Inc., 1984.

Kawamoto, Chizuko. "File Analysis for Retrospective Conversion: The Case of the California State Library, Law Library." *Law Library Journal* 79 (Summer 1987): 455-67.

Lisowski, Andrew. "Vendor-Based Retrospective Conversion at George Washington University." *Library Hi Tech* 1 (Winter 1983): 23-26.

5
Establishing Standards for the Recon Project

In a recon project, you cannot ignore the issue of standards. It has an impact on how the project will be carried out and how the money will be spent. As with many of the decisions with the recon project, it is based on the needs and realities of the specific library and each individual library must determine which standards it will follow in order to achieve its specific objectives. This handbook will raise the various issues concerned with standards, offer some recommendations on standards to be adopted, but cannot cover the specific circumstances of individual libraries. Each library must look at its own needs, resources, and future, and then choose the best set of standards to achieve its goals.

The standards which the library adopts are dictated by the needs of that library. That is one of the reasons why we stressed in an earlier chapter how important it is to determine what your library's precise automation needs are. In the following pages, we are going to look at record format and structure, descriptive and subject cataloging standards, classification schemes, and authority control. For most libraries decisions regarding such standards have already been made and are implemented on a continuing basis. However, with recon the problem of older records causes one to look again at the standards in use in the library and how older records which do not conform to presently used standards are to be handled. In addition to seeing how the choice of various standards are dictated by the needs of the individual library, we are going to see how adherence to, or deviance from, these standards impacts on costs.

Standards to be Considered

Level of Fullness of the Cataloging Record

In most libraries there are probably bibliographic records with varying amounts of bibliographic information. Because of the features of automated library systems and because of the continuing drop in costs for these systems, it is becoming increasingly practical and advantageous for libraries to have as complete bibliographic records as possible. Some of the earlier databases created by libraries and database vendors have short bibliographic records which served specific purposes, such as circulation, or a simple author/title catalog. With the features of some present online catalogs, such as keyword and Boolean searching, a fuller bibliographic record is more useful. If a library doing recon has some short bibliographic records it may be able to upgrade them to full bibliographic records by using a database that has national library cataloging or equivalent standards. Also, if the library is doing recon by direct data entry, it may decide to enhance the short record with more bibliographic information. When deriving records from any source, though, be sure you know the quality of the records there and the fullness of the cataloging. In Chapters 10 through 12 on MARC you will find a list of the bibliographic elements which small- and medium-sized libraries should consider having in their catalogs. When considering the level of fullness of the record, consider the needs of the library, both present and future, and try to build a database which will accommodate future needs. Of course, to some extent there is a price to pay for full bibliographic records. It may require more time now to create the database and the storage costs for full records are more than for short ones. The automated system which the library has, or ultimately chooses, may also have to be more powerful in order to search and retrieve information from more extensive files in an acceptable time, say two to three seconds.

Use of *AACR2*

The issue of *AACR2* in recon is problematic. In the context of recon, we are really more concerned with the choice and structure of headings according to *AACR2*, Chapters 21 through 25, and not so much with the rules which deal with bibliographic description as indicated in Chapters 1 through 13 of *AACR2*. The probability of any library having all its manual catalog records in *AACR2* is small. For the conversion of manual records created after January 1, 1981, there is a good possibility that the records will have been created according to the rules in *AACR2*. However, for the records created prior to that, it is likely that there will be conflict between pre-*AACR2* and *AACR2* headings. In practice, the most that any library can hope for is to have no conflict of headings in its automated catalog, even if some headings are established according to pre-*AACR2* rules. However, if you are deriving records from another database, it is advisable that you know the cataloging code or codes used in that database, whether the database is under authority control, and what impact that will have on your present catalog and its conversion.

Also, you should consider whether choosing not to use *AACR2* now will limit your ability to share your records and acquire records from other libraries in the future. *AACR2* is now a widely accepted cataloging code and every library should seriously consider using it. The cost implications of the use or non-use of *AACR2* are difficult to gauge because they depend so much on the particular catalog. For some libraries the cost of recon will increase if there are a lot of headings to be changed from pre-*AACR2* to *AACR2*. On the other hand, recon carried out by deriving, for example, Library of Congress cataloging, can be an opportunity for a library to upgrade its records to *AACR2* without undue expense of money and staff time.

Use of the MARC Format

The reasons for and against using the MARC format are discussed in greater detail in Chapter 10. In the same way that *AACR2* provides libraries with standards for the content of bibliographic records, MARC provides a standard for communicating machine-readable versions of cataloging records. Use of MARC formats may increase the cost of the recon in terms of purchasing records and training staff to use MARC coding. However, using a MARC format provides important protection for the future by supporting portability of records from one system to the next and the ability to share, exchange, and contribute information to other databases. If the records are obtained from an external source then the local system should be able to accept MARC records. If you wish to contribute records to another system or expect to upgrade the system in the near future then the system holding your recon records should be able to output MARC records.

Use of Subject Access Systems

Subject access in the online catalog has been an issue in recent years and one which will probably be around for some time. While this is not the place to discuss the problems of subject access from a theoretical point of view, the library doing recon must be aware of the problems which subject access systems present in carrying out the project. A great many libraries provide subject access to their collections through the use of a list of subject headings, a thesaurus, or a keyword system. If a library is doing the recon project simply by direct data entry, then there is every possibility that the integrity of the subject access system can be maintained in that no new or obsolete headings will be introduced into the catalog. However, if the library is deriving records from another source, then it is likely that some conflicts will occur between the headings in the derived records and those which the library owns.

Library of Congress Subject Headings (*LCSH*) is the most commonly used list of headings in North American libraries. However, for those libraries that use a different system, such as Sears headings, it will be necessary to edit records derived from a vendor or service bureau, to add or modify the headings contained in the manual record. This will increase the cost of the recon significantly in that every derived record will have to be edited and updated. For those libraries that use *LCSH*, there may be some conflicts between old and new headings, because all subject access systems are changing and evolving over time and not every library can keep abreast of such changes and continually change old headings to new ones. As with *AACR2*, the recon can be an opportunity to acquire more up-to-date subject access at a fraction of the price it would cost to create it. However, whatever your subject access needs are, in the recon project try to match those needs with a cost-effective method of acquiring the machine-readable catalog.

Use of Classification Systems

The classification system used in the library usually will not influence the recon project. This is because the application of a classification number to a work has inevitably been library specific. National library cataloging agencies, however, do provide Library of Congress and Dewey classification numbers for newly created MARC records. Libraries that intend to use national library cataloging on an ongoing basis after the recon project is completed should consider the use of either Dewey or LC classification as the preferred system. For those libraries that are reclassifying their collection at the same time as doing recon, the choice of classification system has to be made, and whether or not the numbers in derived records will be used with or without change.

Use of Authority Control Devices

The most widely used authority control devices in North American libraries are: *Library of Congress Name Authorities, Canadiana Authorities,* and the *Library of Congress Subject Authority File.* Not every library maintains its own authority file, but most libraries have some mechanism for avoiding conflicting headings in their catalog. For the library deriving recon records from a vendor it is important to know if the vendor's database is under authority control—that is, do all headings in the database conform to the headings in an acceptable authority file? It is also important to know if the authority file is the same as the one used in the library. Recon carried out with the use of authority control can reduce the per record cost of recon as less editing is required.

It is possible, however, to have authority control imposed on the project, either during it or after it is completed. In the latter case, the newly created database is matched against a machine-readable authority file, all nonconforming headings are identified and the headings are automatically changed to the authoritative ones. Some libraries may question the need for authority control at all, given that it may not have seemed necessary in their manual environment. With the introduction of online systems, however, it is becoming increasingly obvious that some authority control is necessary to facilitate adequate access to the database. A library, therefore, should first decide if it is going to use authority control, and then decide which authority files it will use.

Checklist:
Establishing Standards for the Recon Project

- level of fullness of the cataloging record
- use of *AACR2*
- use of the MARC format
- use of subject access systems
- use of classification systems
- use of authority control devices

Further Reading

Asher, Richard E. "Retrospective Conversion of Bibliographic Records." *Catholic Library World* 54(November 1982): 155-61.

Boss, Richard W. *Issues in Retrospective Conversion.* N.p.: R.W. Boss, 1985.

Boss, Richard W., and Hal Espo. "Standards, Database Design, & Retrospective Conversion." *Library Journal* 112 (October 1, 1987): 54-58.

Burger, Robert H. "Conversion of Catalog Records to Machine-Readable Form: Major Projects, Continuing Problems, and Future Prospects." *Cataloging & Classification Quarterly* 3 (Fall 1982): 27-40.

Drabenstott, Jon, ed. "Retrospective Conversion: Issues and Perspectives: A Forum." *Library Hi Tech* 4 (Summer 1986): 105-20.

"Guidelines Proposed for Retrospective Conversion of Bibliographic Records of Monographs." *Library of Congress Information Bulletin* 44 (March 25, 1985): 59-60.

"Instant MARC at Cornwall County Library." *Vine* no. 24 (August1978): 17-19.

Intner, Sheila S. "Bibliographic Policies." *Technicalities* 7 (August 1987): 3-6.

Johnson, Carolyn A. "Retrospective Conversion of Three Library Collections." *Information Technology and Libraries* 1 (June 1982): 133-39.

Juneja, Derry C. "Quality Control in Data Conversion." *Library Resources & Technical Services* 31 (April-June 1987): 148-58.

McQueen, Judy, and Richard W. Boss. "Sources of Machine-Readable Cataloging and Retrospective Conversion." *Library Technology Reports* 21 (November-December 1985): 601-732.

Petersen, Karla D. "Planning for Serials Retrospective Conversion." *Serials Review* 10 (Fall 1984): 73-78.

Valentine, Phyllis A., and David R. McDonald."Retrospective Conversion: A Question of Time, Standards, and Purpose." *Information Technology and Libraries* 5 (June 1986): 112-20.

6
Identifying Recon Options

There are a great many recon options available to libraries at the present time. Suppliers of automated services to libraries have realized the quantity of records that remain to be converted and the large amounts of money libraries are willing to spend on the process. So besides a library carrying out its project in isolation, there are many government, not-for-profit, and commercial enterprises involved in the recon business. In order to make an informed choice about how to convert catalog records, you need to be aware of all the options available. In this chapter we discuss four recon options:

- recon done in-house by entering data directly into the library's own database and without any reference to an outside agency
- recon done in-house, making use of external bibliographic resources
- recon done totally by an outside agency on behalf of the library
- blend of in-house and vendor-based recon

Within each group we will examine in general terms the process involved and highlight some of the advantages and disadvantages of each type of option. Appendix I, which provides a snapshot of the services of recon providers, should be used in conjunction with this chapter. Appendix II provides the names, addresses, and telephone numbers of all the services approached for the information contained in Appendix I.

Options Available

In-House Recon

In-house Recon by Direct Data Entry

This option is perhaps the simplest one available to libraries. The process is straightforward. The library enters a copy of the data found in its manual files into a local system, a shared central database, or a utility. Usually the data is derived from the shelf-list, coded to indicate which field the information belongs to in the machine-readable record, and entered into a computer system, thus creating a database. The coding may be done at the time of entry by the data entry operator, or it may be done prior to entry into the system by marking the shelf-list card or creating a worksheet. If the data has been entered into a central database or utility, certain products are usually generated from the system for the library, such as a tape, a microfiche or microfilm copy of its database, or a CD-ROM.

Advantages of direct data entry

The integrity of the manual file can be maintained. By this we mean that no new or extraneous data are introduced into the library's catalog, which could cause conflict of headings, or conflicts with library cataloging policies. The library is not using or accepting someone else's cataloging, but is rather using its own cataloging, however complete or incomplete that might be.

The project may be carried out when staff, time, and funds are available. This consideration is especially important for those libraries that cannot acquire special funds for a recon project but rather must work it into the day-to-day work flow of the library. No commitment of money need be made to an outside agency.

The recon may be completed with only one pass through the shelf-list. Depending on the cataloging policies developed for the recon project, it may not be necessary to seek different or additional information to supplement the shelf-list card. Hence each shelf-list record is dealt with in sequence as found in the shelf-list and procedures for back tracking and subsequent conversion of missed cards are not required.

Avoids vendor charges for loading database. When you buy an automated library system, many vendors charge for formatting and indexing data acquired from other sources, such as from a bibliographic utility. This is because they usually have to do some custom work to their record loading programs, and because if vendors process a database they need to charge for the computer resources used. If records are entered directly into the library's automated system all system vendor involvement is avoided.

Disadvantages of Direct Data Entry

Labor intensive for the library. Recon done in-house by keying in the library's cataloging data is very labor intensive for the library. Coding before data entry and quality control afterwards also have to be considered in calculating the per record cost of the recon.

Coding of data may be required before input. Depending on the qualifications and skills of the staff doing the data entry it may be necessary to code or label the elements of the catalog record before passing it for data entry. For example, you may have to identify and label the author, title, subjects, and other elements of the card. If you are creating MARC records from the cards this step can be quite complex. Some of the worksheets provided as examples in Appendix III have been used for this purpose by libraries embarking on recon with operators who had no previous library experience.

Less opportunity to upgrade the quality of cataloging or move to national standards. The database will only be as good as the information on the original shelf-list cards. It may not be feasible to upgrade and enhance the data to take advantage of improved access that the online catalog will provide, or to improve standards of cataloging.

Online costs may be high. If the recon is being done using a utility then the added cost of online services must be allowed for. In spite of the added cost this may still be a valid option for some libraries, especially when there is a commitment to ongoing use of the utility.

Error checking is essential. Given that all data is typed into the database, it is inevitable that errors in coding and transcription will occur. Such errors impede access to the database and hence supervision and quality control is critical to maintain the standards and usefulness of the database. Such supervision should be done by a regular member of staff, and this added workload should be allowed for by employing temporary back-up staff where necessary.

Extra equipment may have to be purchased. In order to use this option you will have to have selected the automated system and installed the cataloging module, or else have sufficient terminals to connect you to a bibliographic utility, or stand-alone CD-ROM system. Extra equipment, especially terminals, may be needed for the extra staff who are working on the project. However, these terminals can usually be re-assigned to the public access area once the project is completed.

In-house Recon Using an External Resource Database

Another option for libraries doing recon in-house is to obtain machine-readable records from an outside source. In this way the library avoids the necessity of data entry of a large number of records, yet still maintains control of the process and the staffing arrangements. Use of another database as a resource file involves either obtaining a copy of the resource database or having the ability to search the resource database. The process involves searching an outside source for records which match the records in one's shelf-list, making or acquiring copies of the records found, and thus creating the library's database. Local information, such as call number, is copied from the shelf-list to the records acquired in this way. The objective is to find in an external database machine-readable records which match as closely as possible the catalog records in your library. The criteria by which you judge external databases are discussed in the next chapter.

Methods

There are a number of ways of accessing records in an external resource database:

Online. For those libraries that are members of cooperative cataloging agencies, or that make use of the services of a bibliographic utility, there is the possibility of direct online access to the resource database. The process usually requires searching the host database for records which closely match those in the shelf-list. The search terms used depend on the database being searched, with most databases providing access to the records by ISBN, LCCN, author, title, etc. When a matching record is found (a "hit"), the record can be copied to a private file, or transferred directly into the library's system. Local information usually needs to be added to the "derived" record. With this method of recon it is unlikely that a record will be found in the host database for everything in the shelf-list, so normally some direct data entry is also required to complete the conversion of the library's holdings.

Offline or batch mode. There are a number of possibilities for offline access to a resource database, which can be more cost-effective than online methods. Offline charges are usually less than online charges, staff expertise needed for using offline options is usually less than that for online work, and there is greater flexibility in staffing arrangements. The most common methods for offline access to a resource database are:

- Tape. If a library similar to yours already has a machine-readable catalog it may be worth investigating the possibility of obtaining a copy of its database and using it to derive cataloging records for your collection. Use of this option will presuppose that you have the facilities to mount the database on your organization's computer, and that you have the retrieval software necessary to access the records and select the ones you need.

  Alternatively, some organizations, such as the Library of Congress and the National Library of Canada, accept search requests on a tape. Usually the requesting library sends a tape to the database producer in an agreed upon format, using specific search statements, such as ISBN or LCCN. The search requests are then matched against the host database and matching records are identified and extracted. A tape of matching records is returned to the library, where local information can be added. Use of this option also presupposes that you have the facilities to mount the tape on your computer, create the search arguments, and also that you have the retrieval and cataloging software necessary to access the returned records and edit them.

- Paper. Some recon vendors allow you to submit to them search requests, such as ISBNs, on paper and their operators search the database. The database vendor usually returns matched records either on a tape or on floppy diskettes, which the library then processes and edits.

  There have been some efforts made to use the information directly from shelf-list cards using optical character recognition (OCR) systems. On the whole, such efforts have not been very successful because the quality of shelf-list cards has varied so much over the years and the information may have to be coded for fields in the record. It is not a viable option for small or medium-sized libraries. In the early days of recon some vendors also had libraries type search requests using special typefaces which then could be machine-read using OCR equipment. With the advent of the microcomputer, however, such practices have almost disappeared and search requests are now routinely entered onto floppy diskette for machine processing.

- Microcomputer. The advent of the microcomputer has had a great impact on recon in recent years and has made it both more affordable and achievable for smaller libraries. The microcomputer is probably now the most widely used tool in recon and is the common means of access to large databases. The reason for this is that much of the recon work can now be done on an in-house, stand-alone micro-computer, rather than being connected online to a host database. The online charges are significantly reduced and there is much greater flexibility in staffing, as working in off-peak hours is not necessary in order to reduce costs. The two most prevalent ways of gaining access to a resource database are either to create short search re-quests on floppy diskettes or to use CD-ROM.

• Floppy diskettes. With this method of recon a library creates on a floppy dis-kette skeletal bibliographic records, which are subsequently matched against a larg-er database. Using vendor-supplied software, a brief record is created which usually contains the ISBN, LCCN, title, and local information such as call number and notes. The library extracts this information from its shelf-list and the keying of data is done at the convenience of the library. When a diskette is full (500-1,000 records per diskette) it is sent to the resource database and is matched against the full data-base. Matching records are extracted, local information supplied on the floppy dis-kette is added to the record and a copy of the merged record is sent to the library. The copy may be returned to the library on a tape, or floppy diskette, or added to the library's file if it is using a bibliographic utility. Authority control, if available, is an optional extra. By-products of this process usually include a print-out of the records which did not match, and a print-out of any problem records.

• CD-ROM. New technologies are making it possible to install large cataloging databases on CD-ROM at a cataloging workstation. Some CD-ROM systems con-tain the full LC MARC database, while others also contain the holdings of member libraries of consortia. With stand-alone CD-ROM systems, the library searches the database for records which match its shelf-list, adds local information to the records, and thus builds its database. For those records which cannot be found in the database, the system allows the user to create new records from the shelf-list. CD-ROM systems have significantly reduced the cost of recon for some libraries.

Whichever external database is selected, there will inevitably be some "no-hits." These are records for which no match can be found in the resource database. Original records will have to be created for these titles. This can be done after completing the first stage of recon by using an online cataloging module.

The final step, after deriving records from any of these sources, is to load the MARC records that now represent the collection into the automated library system. This will in-volve using a record-loading program provided by the vendor of the library system. Before selecting any of these options it is important to verify that the vendor does in fact have an interface program for loading records from the source that has been chosen.

Advantages of In-House Recon Using an External Resource Database

Captures an existing bibliographic record. This option ensures that the library is cap-turing existing bibliographic information, usually in MARC format. If the resource database is chosen carefully it may also reflect current cataloging standards, such as *AACR2*, and current *LCSH*.

Quality is controlled by the library.   Using a resource database in-house means that the library keeps control over the whole process. In particular, you can monitor the quality of records and adjust policies and procedures if necessary as the project progresses.

No library files leave the library. There is another aspect to the control question, which is that all files stay in the library and there is no need to do without the shelf-list for extended periods or incur the cost of copying it. From the security point of view this is a major advantage.

The recon can start at any time. Assuming that editing software is available the recon can begin before a local automated system is selected or installed by storing the records on floppy diskettes for later loading into the automated system. Alternatively, the file can be built and maintained with a bibliographic utility.

Disadvantages of In-House Recon Using an External Resource Database

Labor intensive. All recon projects are labor intensive, but with this option all the labor will be in-house. This means hiring, training, and managing staff and providing space and resources for them to work with.

Editing of records will be required. Regardless of the source of the records, some editing will be required. A minimum amount of editing is required to add the library's own local information: call number, location, and copy/volume information. In general, records should be accepted "as is," based on having selected this resource database as appropriate for your needs. We can only emphasize once again that recon is not recataloging!

Wide range of costs depending on method chosen. The source of the database will directly affect the cost of obtaining records. Online charges may apply, or the vendor of the records may charge a subscription cost for the database. Obtaining a copy of another library's database for free may turn out to be a false economy if there are hidden costs in setting up computing resources and retrieval software in order to use it.

Wide range in quality of captured records. Part of the selection process in deciding which recon option to adopt involves assessing the quality and appropriateness of the records to your collection. You must be prepared for variation in the quality of records but should not select a source which appears to vary too greatly. Many records in resource databases may not be in full MARC format, nor be cataloged according to *AACR2*. Obsolete subject headings and classification numbers may appear.

May not be able to complete the recon in one pass through the shelf-list. With the exception of the CD-ROM option, you will not know until the matching process is completed which requests produced hits. Therefore you will have to "revisit" the shelf-list cards for those items that did not produce a hit. With the CD-ROM option, the software usually includes the facility to create an original record using a screen worksheet if a hit is not found.

To recap, there are some common advantages and disadvantages to *all types* of *in-house* recon. The advantages are that:

- Quality control remains with the library
- Work is done as staff, time, and funds allow
- Existing staff can be utilized
- No files leave the library
- Staff are familiar with library policies and standards so can solve problems as they arise

On the negative side, you have to consider that:

- Internal staff costs are high
- Additional staff, equipment, and space will be required
- Hiring, training, and managing of project staff are expensive and time consuming
- The recon project will interfere with your staff's regular workload
- The results may be subject to vagaries of the resource database used

Vendor-Based Recon

Most of the bibliographic utilities and several commercial vendors offer full-service recon. This means that they will take your shelf-list and requirements, then using their own staff, equipment, and facilities, create a database from either existing machine-readable records, or create original records from the shelf-list.

There are normally various levels of service offered by the vendors, with each level producing a better quality record and subsequently costing more. It is important that the library choose the level of service which best suits its needs.

The vendors of these services are described in Appendix I. The cost of these services vary considerably and most vendors will wish to quote a price based on having reviewed a sample of your shelf-list.

Advantages of Using an Outside Vendor

The primary advantage of this option is that it moves the recon project out of the library and, consequently, you should have:

Limited library staff involvement. Apart from defining the requirements for the recon project and liaison with the vendor, the involvement of the library staff should be much less than with the in-house option. A senior member of staff who is very familiar with the library's cataloging procedures and policies should be assigned the task of working with the vendor. The same person should also be documenting the procedures the vendor is to follow, interpreting the information that will be found on shelf-list cards, and establishing the requirements for the level of information to be created.

Specific costs are known in advance. As mentioned above, the vendor will usually quote a fixed price for the project based on a review of sample shelf-list cards. The only unknown cost will be for staff involvement in liaison with the vendor and quality control once the records are received at the library.

No additional outlay for equipment or facilities is required. By moving the recon out of the library you can avoid having to set up a special area and equipment for temporary staff and the recon project.

Minimizes project staff recruitment or training. Obtaining and managing temporary staff for a project such as recon takes the time of regular staff throughout the life of the project. In many cases this can be a full-time job. Use of an external service bureau avoids this expense.

Specific time frame for completion of the project. Along with a fixed price for the project, the vendor should also be committed to a specific delivery date. While this is hard to cast in stone for any project involving computers, it is possible to build in a level of protection by contracting the payment schedule based on delivery of the finished product and penalties for not meeting the agreed deadlines.

Disadvantages of Using an Outside Vendor

Less quality control. Allowing operators outside the library to create the records means that, to some extent, you lose control of the quality of the records. It is important to sample records as they are returned and loaded into your automated system. However, it is impossible to look at every record, and this would defeat the purpose of hiring an outside agency in the first place. Selection of a particular vendor must be based on having confidence that the records provided will be suitable.

Files may leave the library. With this option the shelf-list is normally shipped to the vendor. The library may decide that it cannot continue normal operations without a shelf-list and therefore incurs the cost of copying or microfilming the shelf-list before shipping it. Copying the shelf-list is also an important insurance against loss or damage while it is off the premises.

Liaison, follow-up, and editing required. The amount of involvement by library staff varies greatly. It is a factor of how complicated the library's requirements are, how effective and efficient the vendor is, and how much post-load editing is required. In a successful project all of these will be kept to a minimum; however, this is not always the case in the real world and an unexpected amount of follow-up and editing may be required.

Blend of In-House and Vendor-Based Recon

For some libraries it may be useful to consider a blend of in-house and vendor-based recon. In this case a library would use its own staff and resources for the conversion of some of its records and then contract out to an outside vendor those parts of the collection which it is not feasible to convert itself. For example, a library may decide that it will use the LC MARC file on CD-ROM for the conversion of its post-1967 records and then have a vendor convert all the pre-1968 records. The advantage to this method of recon is that the library allocates its resources to the best advantage, using its own staff where appropriate and cost-effective, and using an outside vendor when it becomes most useful.

Conclusion

This chapter has presented an overview of the recon options available to libraries. Each library embarking on recon should explore further in a more practical way the services offered by the vendors indicated in Appendix I, and also any other vendors available to a particular library which are not listed here. The next chapter provides some guidelines for analyzing the options available to you, so that you can narrow down the choices and identify the ones most appropriate to your situation.

Checklist:
Identifying Recon Options

In-House Recon

- Direct data entry
- Use of external resource database
  - Online
  - Off-line
    - Tape
    - Paper
    - Microcomputer
      - Floppy diskette
      - CD-ROM

Vendor-Based Recon

- Full service
- Levels of service

Blend of In-House and Vendor-Based Recon

Further Reading

Baldwin, Paul E., and Leigh Swain. *RECON Alternatives for Eight British Columbia Public Libraries: An Ancillary Report for the British Columbia Library Network. Prepared at the Request of the Greater Vancouver Library Federation and Greater Victoria Public Library.* Richmond, BC: British Columbia Union Catalogue, 1980.

Beaumont, Jane. "Retrospective Conversion on a Micro: Options for Libraries." *Library Software Review* 5 (July-August 1986): 213-18.

Bocher, Robert. "MITINET: Catalog Conversion to a MARC Database." *School Library Journal* 31 (March 1985): 109-12.

Desmarais, Norman. "BiblioFile for Retrospective Conversion." *Small Computers in Libraries* 5 (December 1985): 24-28.

Douglas, Nancy E. "REMARC Retrospective Conversion: What, Why, and How." *Technical Services Quarterly* 2 (Spring-Summer 1985): 11-16.

Drabenstott, Jon, ed. "Retrospective Conversion: Issues and Perspectives: A Forum." *Library Hi Tech* 4 (Summer 1986): 105-20.

Epstein, Hank. "MITINET/retro: Retrospective Conversion on an Apple." *Information Technology and Libraries* 2 (June 1983): 166-73.

_____. "A System for Retrospective Conversion." *American Libraries* 15 (February 1984): 113-14.

Harrison, Martin. "Retrospective Conversion of Card Catalogues into Full MARC Format Using Sophisticated Computer-Controlled Visual Imaging Techniques." *Program* 19 (July 1985): 213-30.

Hoare, Peter A. "Retrospective Catalogue Conversion in British University Libraries: A Survey and a Discussion of Problems." *British Journal of Academic Librarianship* 1 (Summer 1986): 95-131.

Information Systems Consultants Inc. *Retrospective Conversion for the Libraries of McGill University.* N.p.: Information Systems Consultants Inc., 1984.

"Machine-Readable Cataloging Data Providers." *Library Systems Newsletter* 5 (November 1985): 86-88.

MacMillan, Gary D. "UTLAS DISCON: REMARC/MARC on CD-ROM in Hawaii." *CD-ROM Librarian* 2 (September-October 1987): 12-15.

McGill University. Libraries/Systems Office. *Summary of a New Method for RECON.* Montreal: The Office, 1985.

McQueen, Judy, and Richard W. Boss. "Sources of Machine-Readable Cataloging and Retrospective Conversion." *Library Technology Reports* 21 (November-December 1985): 601-732.

Purnell, Kathleen M. "Productivity in a Large-Scale Retrospective Conversion Project." In *Productivity in the Information Age: Proceedings of the 46th ASIS Annual Meeting 1983,* edited by Raymond F. Vondran, Anne Caputo, Carol Wasserman, and Richard A.V. Diener. White Plains, NY: Knowledge Industry Publications, Inc. for the American Society for Information Science, 1983.

"RECON and REMARC at Edinburgh University Library." *Vine* 49 (August 1983): 13-18.

Reed-Scott, Jutta. "Retrospective Conversion: An Update." *American Libraries* 16 (November 1985): 694, 696, 698.

Reed-Scott, Jutta, Dorothy Gregor, and Charles Payne. *Issues in Retrospective Conversion: Report of a Study Conducted for the Council on Library Resources.* Washington, DC: Council on Library Resources, 1984.

"Retrospective Conversion." *Information Technology and Libraries* 3 (September 1984): 267-78, 280-84, 286-92.

Richardson, Valerie. "Retrospective Conversion Using LYNX and REMARC." *LASIE* 14 (September-October 1983): 14-25.

Ross, John, and Bruce Royan. "Backfile Conversion Today: CIM era or Chimera?" *Program* 11 (October 1977): 156-65.

Severtson, Susan. "REMARC: A Retrospective Conversion Project." *Program* 17 (October 1983): 224-32.

Smith, Sharon, Robert Watkins, and Shirley Richardson. "Retrospective Conversion of Serials at the University of Houston: Midterm Report." *Serials Librarian* 9 (Spring 1985): 63-68.

Watkins, Deane. "Record Conversion at Oregon State." *Wilson Library Bulletin* 60 (December 1985): 31-33.

7
Analyzing the Options

Deciding which recon option is right for you is a question of weighing a number of issues and balancing these against the funds and resources you have available for the project. First, there are the practical considerations: the resources the library has to commit to the project; the current state of the library catalog; and the library's requirements and needs in creating an online database. The characteristics and requirements of the vendors of machine-readable records also have to be considered. Against these considerations you have to determine the relative costs of records and services.

All of these issues are interrelated. One way to assess what each recon option means to you is to create a chart with rows for each of the considerations listed below, and columns for each recon option that you are interested in. Then look at each option and note how it will affect the library for each of the issues to be considered. This will help you to systematically gather information and reach a conclusion about what is best for your situation.

Practical Considerations

Library Resources

The first consideration is the resources the library has to devote to the recon project. Staff, equipment, space, time, and money will all be required. The amount or type of resources the library has in each of these areas will have a strong influence on the option chosen. For example, if the library has funds, but not equipment or space for the project, it would make most sense to choose an option that uses a service bureau and moves the project out of the library. On the other hand, if you have funds available for staff but not for services, then you will select an in-house option. You need to consider each of the following resource requirements to decide which approach is feasible in your library, and what the implications are for you.

Staff. Does the library have the staff resources available to take on this project? Extra staff will be required, whichever option is selected. Recon should not be treated as a project to be done in the spare time of regular staff. Depending on the option selected, and the magnitude of the project, the library may need staff for coding, data entry, quality control and proofreading, supervision, and management.

A library staff member should supervise the project to interpret local cataloging policies and to ensure continuity throughout the project. In order to relieve him or her for this project, consideration should be given to hiring back-up staff for some day-to-day operations.

Equipment. What equipment is required for each option and do you have the resources to provide for the work that has to be done in the library? If the option involves buying special equipment, e.g., a CD-ROM drive, does the library have a use for it after the project is completed?

Every option requires some equipment and this will probably involve allocating funds to purchase it and ensuring that it can be properly disposed of or re-assigned after the project is over.

Location. The in-house option, in particular, involves providing space for the project. Lack of space in your library may preclude selecting this option and require you to consider getting the recon done by an external agency. The space allocated for an in-house recon project should be in the library where it can be properly supervised and day-to-day problems can be dealt with efficiently.

Time. By the time the recon project is completed it will have required large amounts of many people's time. From planning to execution there will be management time involved in selecting the appropriate option, setting up the project, and managing it on an ongoing basis. However hard you try to isolate the project from the day-to-day operations there will inevitably be problems that can only be solved by experienced staff. Such problem solving can be very disruptive to regular operations and must be allowed for in planning the recon project.

Also, time limits must be put on the project in terms of setting realistic goals and milestones for the recon team. These goals may be imposed by external conditions, such as the need to implement online circulation before the start of an academic year, or self-imposed to ensure the project does not drag on indefinitely.

Funds available. This will be one of the major influences in the selection of an option. There may be constraints on how you can spend the funds available. For example, funds may be available from a special source for hiring local personnel but very little available for spending with a vendor. This scenario would tend to dictate an in-house project, whereas lack of local, qualified personnel would point towards using a service bureau if the funds are available.

Before starting to evaluate the recon options determine what funds are available and decide whether there are constraints which should lead you to reject some options immediately.

In determining funding options some libraries may be able to take advantage of job creation and training funds for special projects. Database creation is an ideal project for this as it provides training and experience in computer operation and data processing. Sources of funds and training courses in your state or province should be investigated.

Library Catalogs

As we have previously emphasized, the recon project should not be considered an opportunity to recatalog the collection. However, reviewing the following issues will help you to assess whether you should be looking at external sources of records or not.

Quality and consistency of the existing catalog records. The level and quality of cataloging in the library has often varied over the years and the recon project is a good opportunity to obtain records which conform to national standards and provide more complete information than is presently available in some catalogs.

The library's current practices in authority control also have to be considered. There are a number of options for introducing authority control to an online catalog after the recon project and these are discussed in Chapter 9. If the present card catalog has been maintained under careful authority control it may be more appropriate to rely on the existing cards rather than deriving records externally.

Uniqueness. The uniqueness of your library's collection will have a bearing on whether it is appropriate to go to an external source for records or to rely on the information in the shelf-list. Checking a representative sample of the shelf-list against potential sources of records will provide you with an estimate of how high the matching or hit rate will be. An 80 to 90 percent hit rate is usually considered very good. A hit rate of 60 to 80 percent would be considered above average and adequate to consider that source of records seriously. Below 60 percent it may not be worth obtaining externally derived records unless there are other compelling reasons, such as the need to upgrade records or minimize in-house data entry.

Standards. What standards does the library presently adhere to? The standards currently used, such as *AACR2*, and those that you wish to introduce into the catalog should be considered. If the library already owns some records in MARC format, then the recon records should also conform to that.

Quantity. The number of records to be converted will have a bearing on the option selected. As discussed previously, as good an estimate as possible should be made of the records to be converted. Without that estimate it is very difficult to estimate the resources required to complete the project.

Library Requirements

There are certain factors that the library must maintain control over no matter how the recon is done. These include:

Quality control. Whichever recon option is chosen the library must be able to sample records regularly and consistently to ensure that the project is proceeding as expected, and to detect problems before they become major ones. It is important to state the quality control requirements in writing and to establish procedures for regularly sampling the results of the project.

Standards. This is one of the first items that should be established when looking at recon options. First, list the standards that are presently established for cataloging at your library. This should include the cataloging rules, the classification schedules, the subject headings, and any other standards relevant to special materials in your collection. In assessing options for recon you should be checking whether records will adhere to current standards or be in conflict with them. Finally, having established standards for the catalog records the library must have confidence that these standards will be maintained during the project. The standards should be documented and included in everyone's procedure manual.

Cost control. The library needs to know what it will be receiving for its funds. What services will be provided within the scope of the project, and what will not be covered? In assessing the various options for recon consider whether an option provides fixed price for the project or is an open-ended estimate. If it is open ended then there must be a way of monitoring and controlling costs to ensure that the project is completed within the expected budget.

Portability of records. The library's need for transferring records to other systems in the future should be considered. The possible reasons for needing to transfer records are discussed in the chapters of this book on MARC. The minimum requirement is that the library be able to transfer the database to another system in the future, should that become necessary or desirable.

Vendor Characteristics

Having dealt with the practical considerations from the library point of view, it is time to carefully assess the vendor options. The issues related to selection of a vendor concern the type, quality, and quantity of not only the records that are offered to libraries, but also the services. There is no advantage to selecting a vendor with a superior database of records to draw upon if the services offered are inappropriate, inadequate, or too costly.

Database. The first consideration should be the database of records that the vendor works with in providing records to libraries for recon purposes. The goal of a library in using an outside vendor for MARC records is to obtain the highest hit rate from a single source as inexpensively as possible. Ideally the library should be looking for a vendor who can match at least 80 to 85 percent of the cards in the shelf-list. In order to establish a hit rate most vendors will accept a representative sample of the shelf-list and test this against the database. You should select a sample of 100 to 200 records which represent the full range of materials in your library from the point of view of publication dates, types of materials, and subject matter. Careful selection of the sample will allow you to gain the best estimate of a vendor's applicability to your needs, and to compare competing services equitably.

Another consideration when reviewing outside resource records is the subject coverage of the database. A public, school, or college library will probably be best served by large, general purpose databases, such as those that the CD-ROM products and bibliographic utilities provide. A special library will have to select more carefully and try to match its needs with a vendor who holds records from similar types of libraries. Again, a hit rate test on the shelf-list will guide you in selecting a vendor who covers your subject matter adequately.

The source of records is also important. The vendor database will be richer if it includes user records in addition to source records from the national resource libraries. However, if you will be using a large number of user records, it is important to be confident that the contributed records meet your requirements in terms of standards.

Finally, is the database available in MARC format? All the vendors listed in the appendix provide records in MARC format, since this is the established format for communicating records between automated library systems. However, there may be a neighboring library, with a similar collection, which is willing to let you use its system to build a database by deriving from their records. If you enter into an arrangement like that it is essential to ensure that the records you derive can be extracted from the database in MARC format. If this is not possible you may become involved in unexpected expenses for special programming to extract your records and load them into your system.

Coverage. The years that the database covers must also be considered. LC MARC records were first introduced in 1968. Therefore the coverage in many databases for earlier years is selective and very incomplete. If your library contains many older materials it will be necessary to find a vendor who can either offer records contributed by users with similar collections, or who has access to the alternative files.

Quality and consistency. The quality of cataloging in the records that vendors offer can vary enormously. This is why it is important to know the source of the records. In general you can rely on records that are contributed by national libraries. These libraries, along with the major research and academic libraries, usually have the highest standards of cataloging. In selecting a vendor you should be looking for one whose records match, or improve upon, the quality of your cataloging.

The wider the range of sources of records the more likely you are to obtain records with inconsistent headings and these inconsistencies will show up when the records are loaded into your automated system. If there are likely to be a number of inconsistent headings introduced into the database through recon, then it may be expedient to consider one of the authority control services as a final step in database building. The issue of authority control is discussed in Chapter 13—MARC Authority Records and in Chapter 14—Editing Derived Records.

Uniqueness. The more specialized your library, the more carefully you will have to review the vendor offerings to find a suitable match of records and an adequate hit rate.

Quantity. The size of resource databases varies enormously. In addition, the total number of available records claimed by the vendor may be misleading. A more accurate gauge of the quantity of records available is the total number of unique records in the database. Some shared cataloging systems may maintain duplicate but essentially identical records, for each library holding a title. In that case there is little to be gained from trying to match your recon requests against the largest database available. In practice, the coverage and quality of records in a resource database should be a higher priority in selecting a vendor than quantity of records available.

Standards. When considering standards from the vendor point of view you are interested in whether the vendor requires you to adhere to certain standards, or whether the library is entitled to derive records and edit them at will to reflect their standards and practices. In general you want to find a vendor that will provide records that meet accepted international standards but provides the facility for editing to meet local requirements.

Customer service. The vendors of bibliographic records offer a wide range of customer support services. These range from little or nothing, through telephone help only, to on-site training and provision of an "800" line for follow-up calls and questions. It is important to ascertain the level of support available from your preferred vendor and to assess whether it is adequate and appropriate for your needs.

Vendor requirements

When you select an outside vendor for the project the vendor will probably have some requirements for dealing with your records.

Files. If the recon is to be done externally, the shelf-list cards will probably have to be submitted to the vendor's offices. This means you will be without the shelf-list for ongoing cataloging for an extended period of time. Can the library continue to operate without the shelf-list or should a copy be made before submitting the cards to the vendor? If the cards are sent off-site then insurance coverage should be arranged and the contract should state clearly who is responsible for the safety and security of the cards during this time.

The vendor may also have some requirements as to how the cards are to be divided into batches and/or edited before submission. The time and effort involved in preparing cards for the vendor should be included in the budget and schedule for the project.

Costs. Vendors who provide recon services will have a range of charges depending on how much human intervention is involved in the process of selecting records and editing them to match the library's requirements. The amount that the library is prepared to pay to the vendor will be determined by the funds available and the resources in the library to support the recon project.

The payment schedule to the vendor also needs to be determined and agreed upon with a contract that spells out how many records will be delivered, at what cost, and when payments should be made.

Schedule. Since the vendor is receiving recon projects from a variety of sources they may need to schedule your work several months in advance. It is important to determine their schedule and negotiate to reach a mutually agreeable timetable.

Copyright. This has been a thorny issue over the past ten years. Who owns the machine-readable records that the vendor has created for your bibliographic database? What right do you have to share or redistribute those records after they have been loaded into your automated library system? Some vendors have attempted to put copyright on the records supplied through their services and to limit the library's right to share those records in a network or consortium.

The library should have the right to use its records however it wishes. This issue needs to be clarified at the start of the project and agreed upon in the service contract between the library and the vendor.

Determining Costs

Costs

The cost components of the recon project break down into three groups: staffing, equipment and supplies, and vendor services or utility charges. How and where funds are spent on these items will depend on how much each option allows you to do the recon in-house and/or require you to purchase external services.

Staff. Staff costs will involve the additional staff hired to work at the library for the duration of the project and also any back-up support that is to be provided in order to relieve existing staff of regular duties during the project.

Equipment and supplies. This includes any microcomputers, terminals, printers, and consumable supplies that may be needed. The cost of telecommunications and equipment maintenance services should also be considered.

Vendor or utility charges. There will be charges for external services if any of the service bureau options are selected. These will generally be on a per record basis so the total can be calculated by multiplying by the expected rate of return in matching records.

How to Determine Costs

Overall costs can be calculated for each option under consideration by following the steps described below. Costs should be determined as accurately as possible so that different options can be compared properly. The best way to compare the cost of various options is on a per record basis. After determining all the costs for the project, the per record cost is derived by dividing the total cost by the total number of records to be converted.

Choose appropriate options. By this stage you should have identified one or two recon options that seem most appropriate for you. These should be the ones that you select for more detailed comparison of costs.

Identify cost variables for each option. For each option under review you should identify the components of the project that require funds. These will vary in amounts but will be a combination of the items discussed previously: staff, equipment and supplies, and services.

Establish representative sample from shelf-list. If you have not already done so you should select a sample of 100 to 200 cards from the shelf-list that represents the range of your collection in terms of subject matter, imprint dates, and language. This sample will be used to determine the amount of time it will take staff to prepare cards and convert them. The hit rate against various resource databases can also be determined using this sample.

Compare sample with each option. After selecting a representative sample from the shelf-list, these cards should used to compare each option. The time taken to enter the information in a direct data entry project can be measured and used to calculate the total resources required for conversion. Similarly, a hit rate test on a resource database and the time taken to derive and edit records will give an indication of the results that will be achieved on the whole catalog. When comparing hit rate tests, you must also calculate the cost of dealing with the no-hits by some other method, such as direct data entry.

Walk through each option step by step. Using the sample cards you can walk through each step in the different options that you are comparing. Vendors should be willing to do the hit rate test for you and give you an indication of the expected success rate for deriving records from their resource database. When you are doing this "walk through" it is important to include the preparatory steps, quality control, and follow-up that will be required; do not simply cost the project based on data entry or vendor charges.

Determine for each step the staff, equipment and supplies, and vendor costs. Finally, with the information gathered by converting the sample under each option, derive the per record cost to provide you with equivalent figures for cost comparison.

In reality, overall costs may not vary that much for the different options we have described. The differences lie in where the funds are spent and how much appears to be hidden by using existing resources. Some libraries and vendors will claim that recon can be done for less than $1 per record. We believe that $2 and up is a more realistic figure if you take into account the hidden costs, such as existing staff time to supervise and manage the project, the loss of time for current cataloging while staff deal with problems, and liaison with the recon vendor. This is not to say that a recon should not be done, simply that it is important to be realistic about the costs and effort involved so that you and your management are comfortable that the benefits justify the costs.

Checklist:
Analyzing the Options

Practical Considerations

Library Resources

- Staff
- Equipment
- Location
- Time
- Funds available

Library Catalogs

- Quality and consistency of the existing catalog records
- Uniqueness
- Standards
- Quantity

Library Requirements

- Quality control
- Standards
- Cost control
- Portability of records

Vendor Characteristics

- Database
- Coverage
- Quality and consistency
- Uniqueness
- Quantity
- Standards
- Customer service

Vendor Requirements

- Files
- Costs
- Schedule
- Copyright

Determining Costs

Costs

- Staff
- Equipment and supplies
- Vendor or utility charges

How to Determine Costs

- Choose appropriate options
- Identify cost variables for each option
- Establish representative sample from the shelf-list
- Compare sample with each option
- Walk through each option step by step
- Determine for each step the staff, equipment and supplies, and vendor costs

Further Reading

Asher, Richard E. "Retrospective Conversion of Bibliographic Records." *Catholic Library World* 54(November 1982): 155-61.

Auld, Lawrence W. S. "Retrospective Catalog Conversion Costs." Chap. 15 in *Electronic Spreadsheets for Libraries*. Phoenix, AZ: Oryx Press, 1986.

Boss, Richard W. *Issues in Retrospective Conversion*. N.p.: R. W. Boss, 1985.

Boss, Richard W., and Hal Espo. "Standards, Database Design, & Retrospective Conversion." *Library Journal* 112 (October 1, 1987): 54-58.

Carter, Ruth C., and Scott Bruntjen. *Data Conversion*. Professional Librarian Series. White Plains, NY: Knowledge Industry Publications, 1983.

Hoare, Peter A. "Retrospective Catalogue Conversion in British University Libraries: A Survey and a Discussion of Problems." *British Journal of Academic Librarianship* 1 (Summer 1986): 95-131.

Miller, Bruce Cummings. "Spreadsheet Models of Library Activities." *Library Hi Tech* 1 (Spring 1984): 19-25.

" 'Ownership' of Machine-Readable Records: A Neglected Consideration in Retrospective Conversion." *Library Systems Newsletter* 4 (June 1984): 43-46.

Peters, Stephen H., and Douglas J. Butler. "A Cost Model for Retrospective Conversion Alternatives." *Library Resources & Technical Services* 28 (April-June 1984): 149-51, 154-62.

Ricker, Karina. "A Geac Library's Experience with Microcon." *RTSD Newsletter* 12 (Fall 1987): 44-46.
Valentine, Phyllis A., and David R. McDonald."Retrospective Conversion: A Question of Time, Standards, and Purpose." *Information Technology and Libraries* 5 (June 1986): 112-20.

8
Choosing an Option

By the time you reach this point in the project you should have determined the library's needs, established parameters and standards for the project, and analyzed the options and resources available for successful completion of recon. Now you have to make the final decision about how the recon is going to be done and who is going to do it.

Ideal Situation

The ideal situation in choosing an option would be to obtain a machine-readable catalog at the lowest possible cost, with the highest quality records, and having little or no impact on current library operations. As you can imagine this does not happen in the real world. In reality you have to make compromises between cost, quality, and impact in order to have a viable project. A few comments are in order about each of these factors:

Lowest Cost

In recon services, as in most other purchases, you get what you pay for. The minimum cost recon would be to hire data entry staff and enter information directly from the shelf-list. This means you will not be upgrading the cataloging information and may have compromised on quality of records, and impact on the library.

Similarly, on the cost issue, the lowest bid from a vendor may not necessarily be the best one. You should check carefully with other libraries who have used the vendor's services to see if they were satisfied with the hit rate and quality of records received. If you do decide to take the lowest bid make sure you know exactly what you will and will not be getting. For example, the cheapest records may not include editing to merge your local call number, location, and holdings information, so there will have to be a follow-up in-house project to enter that information from the shelf-list.

The lowest cost option may also have a high administrative overhead and this should not be forgotten. An in-house project or low-cost vendor option may require more management and administrative resources, ultimately saving little over a higher cost vendor option.

Highest Quality

If the quality of cataloging and following established national standards are more important than the overall cost of the project, then you can afford to identify and buy the best quality records, and introduce authority control to standardize and upgrade the records to current cataloging practices. Following established national standards does cost money and this is often where compromises are made. It is important to assess the eventual uses of the records and your needs before compromising too far in this area. If the records are to be included in regional union catalogs, then it may be more important to maintain standards than if the records are strictly for in-house use.

Minimal Impact on Library

Every recon project has an impact on the library. The normal workflow of the library may be disrupted because files are in use for special purposes, and the regular staff may be asked to deal with problems. Management staff will have to be relieved of other duties for the duration of the project in order to manage it. The amount of disruption the library can absorb will have a bearing on whether the project is done in-house or contracted out to a vendor.

The Real Situation

As you can imagine, the real situation in selecting a recon option is likely to be a compromise between cost, quality, and impact. That is why it is important to know your needs, understand the standards issue, and realize the options available before making the choice.

The choice is yours, because every library's needs and resources differ. We hope that by systematically reviewing the issues involved in the choice we have helped you to make this first, important step in doing a recon project.

Checklist:
Choosing an Option

Ideal Situation

- Lowest cost
- Highest quality
- Minimal impact on library

Real Situation

- Compromise between cost, quality and impact

Further Reading

Hein, Morten. "Optical Scanning for Retrospective Conversion of Information." *Electronic Library* 4 (December 1986): 328-31.

Hoadley, Irene B., and Leila Payne. "Toward Tomorrow: A Retrospective Conversion Project." *Journal of Academic Librarianship* 9 (July 1983): 138-41.

Lisowski, Andrew. "Vendor-Based Retrospective Conversion at George Washington University." *Library Hi Tech* 1 (Winter 1983): 23-26.

Lisowski, Andrew, and Judith Sessions. "Selecting a Retrospective Conversion Vendor." *Library Hi Tech* 1 (Spring 1984): 65-68.

"OCLC, AMIGOS and SOLINET Retrospective Conversion." *Library Hi Tech News* no. 13 (February 1985): 5-6.

"OCR-Based Retrospective Conversion." *Library Systems Newsletter* 5 (January 1985): 1-2.

9
Developing an Action Plan for Recon

Before actually getting down to work on the recon project, library management and the recon project manager must develop a plan of action. Many of the issues discussed here will already have been considered in connection with selecting a recon option. Now that the decision has been made, it is time to develop an action plan that will bring you to the point where you are ready to start the actual creation of machine-readable data. The details of implementing a recon project and MARC coding in your library are further discussed in Chapter 13: Implementation and Project Management.

The more thorough the preparatory work, the more smoothly the actual recon will go. Careful planning at this stage will ensure that vendor and/or library staff time is not wasted on dealing with too many unforseen problems or details. Another valuable result of this exercise will be a definitive list of the resources required to complete the project in terms of staff, funds, equipment, supplies, external services, and space.

Considerations

Assign Supervisory Staff

If you have not already done so, a project manager should be appointed. This person will have overall responsibility for the management, scheduling, and monitoring of the recon project. In a small library this may well be the chief librarian; in other cases a member of the library management team should be appointed. In addition to managing the day-to-day operations of the recon, the project manager should be responsible for liaison with any vendors and suppliers involved in the project.

If an in-house recon option has been selected and the library wishes to maximize its investment in special equipment and minimize the time taken to do the recon, then two or more shifts of staff may be scheduled for each day. In this case there needs to be a shift supervisor for each shift so that continuity can be maintained and small problems dealt with promptly. There should be at least one occasion each week when the supervisors can meet together to share information. An alternative to weekly meetings is the establishment of a project diary or log as a way of communicating questions, answers, and progress reports.

The first task of the project manager should be the preparation of a policies and procedures manual, which will serve as a record of the decisions that have been made in the process of selecting a recon option and as a user manual for those staff involved in the day-to-day operations of the recon project.

Establish Written Policies

In the process of deciding which recon option the library is going to use, you will have made a number of policy decisions about the extent and type of recon that will be carried out. These decisions should be written down and circulated to everyone who is involved in the project. Policy statements will cover such issues as the parameters of the project:

- which catalog records are to be converted
- how much editing will done on derived records
- how much reclassification and/or recataloging is to be done
- under what circumstances reclassification and/or recataloging is to be carried out
- the intended use of the converted records

Policy decisions may also have been made on some related library activities. For example:

- closing and discarding the card catalog
- maintenance of the existing shelf-list
- weeding and inventory control prior to conversion

The library's requirements and policies for successful completion of the recon should also be recorded. These will include decisions on such matters as:

- quality control procedures
- standards for cataloging rules, classification schedules, subject headings, and machine-readable record formats
- expansion of abbreviations included in present catalog cards
- cost control measures

Apart from the value of having written policies available during the project, it is equally important to have a historical record of the decisions that were made. Many librarians involved in recon at the moment are probably wishing that they had a record of cataloging department decisions over the life of the manual card catalog. Starting that policy record with the commencement of automation will serve the library well in long-range planning for library automation.

Produce Detailed Procedure Manuals for Staff

The second part of a recon manual should be a detailed procedure manual for the staff involved in the project. The library's own version of the tasks described in the implementation of a recon project (Chapter 13) need to be described for staff. Depending on the familiarity of recon staff with library functions and jargon, you may need to cover some or all of the following topics:

- the reasons for, and benefits of, catalog conversion
- a definition of basic library and cataloging terms
- the parts of a catalog card record and the equivalent fields in a machine-readable record
- use of the selected software and equipment
- data entry procedures
- file and diskette management and back-ups on microcomputers
- proofreading and quality control
- management of batches of cards

Procedures for the project manager and/or supervisors also need to be recorded. These will include information about the management of:

- operator training for coding the cards and data entry
- preparation of batches of cards from the shelf-list
- diskettes and equipment assigned to operators
- troubleshooting and problem solving
- handling exceptions in the shelf-list batches
- quality control and follow-up
- tracking totals to ensure all records are converted and loaded into the automated system
- scheduling and staffing on each shift
- rotation of duties among operators
- communications with management, vendor, and operators

Determine Staffing Requirements

Preparing the policies and procedures manual will help you clarify what has to be done to accomplish the recon project. It will now be easier to decide exactly what the staffing requirements for the project will be. Bearing in mind any previously identified constraints, such as time, training facilities, and the source and amount of funds available, you should now identify how many additional staff are required on a contract basis, the skills required, and the amount of time supervision of the project will take for existing staff.

The skills needed for this project will vary depending on the task. For example, the in-house recon option may require data entry operators with fast, accurate typing skills, some knowledge of terminal operations, and a basic understanding of cataloging information. Supervisors will need a higher level of knowledge about microcomputers, the software being used, and cataloging rules in order to deal with problems and train new operators. If the library has decided to work with the MARC communications format then different levels of understanding of MARC will be required by members of the team.

Some of these skills can be learned on-the-job as part of the start-up training period—for example, the basic understanding of cataloging and library functions. Other skills, such as fast, accurate typing and microcomputer experience, may be a basic qualification for the job.

Determine Training Requirements and Identify Resources Available

Adequate training is an important component of a successful recon project. Staff involved in the project must not only know what they are doing, but also have an understanding of why the recon is being undertaken and its relationship to overall library operations and automation. Placing the recon in context will allow staff to make more informed decisions at all levels, and give them a sense of ownership of—and pride in—the quality of the final product.

Some training, such as background information on library operations and automation, can be provided by existing staff as part of a general orientation program. Hands-on training for coding shelf-list cards and operating equipment may be provided by the project manager or by a vendor who is supplying services, software, or equipment. The library may also need to purchase some training from local sources, such as a community college or board of education.

In order to determine training requirements and the resources available, it may help to create a chart of all the people involved in the project, their existing skills, skills needed for their assigned tasks in the recon project, and potential sources for acquiring needed skills. Having made that skills inventory, it will be possible to assess the time and funds that will be required to acquire the necessary skills.

Determine Requirements for External Services

Whichever recon option is chosen you will almost certainly need to obtain some services from external sources. These will include training and equipment maintenance or repair, in addition to those from the vendor of bibliographic records. These requirements need to be assessed and priced so that the costs can be included in the final budget and contracts can be drawn up.

Establish Timetable and Task Lists

Each of the steps described above represent sequential, dependent considerations that must be made in order to develop the final task list and establish a timetable for the project. By the time you reach this point it should be relatively easy to list the tasks that have to be completed, allocate the resources and decide how much time will be required for each step.

Allocate All Necessary Resources to the Project

Funds. In Chapter 7 we discussed the preparation of a detailed budget and now, having developed the schedule, it will be possible to tell funding agencies when funds will be required, how the money will be spent, and how much will be needed in each installment. You probably would not have reached this point in a recon project without some previous commitment to funding; however at this stage you allocate the financial resources so that their use can be properly applied and monitored.

Staff. With the funding assured and plans for the recon in place, you can now hire extra staff and allocate internal staff resources to the project. In recruiting staff for data entry and other jobs, be prepared to administer basic tests to applicants in order to ensure that staff have adequate, accurate typing skills and pay careful attention to detail.

Work location. Adequate space for the recon team to work in is very important and may not be readily available in smaller libraries. Ideally, an in-house recon should be carried out in the technical services area or workroom so that the shelf-list is not removed from those needing it on an ongoing basis. Accomodating a recon team may require some reorganization of space in the workroom and lack of space in the library may have been one of the deciding factors in contracting with an external vendor for recon.

In addition to space, the data entry operators need appropriate desks and chairs for their workstation areas since they will be spending extended periods sitting at the terminal or microcomputer. Ergonomically sound work areas are one of the essential factors in maintaining momentum and enthusiasm for a task that eventually becomes routine and repetitive.

Equipment and supplies. Necessary equipment and supplies should be obtained and installed prior to the actual start of the project and arrival of staff. After installation of hardware and software the project manager and supervisors should test all equipment and software to ensure that you have functional, working systems.

With the action plan in place and resources allocated to the project you should be in a position to start conversion of the catalog. The next three chapters (Chapters 10–12) are intended to provide an appropriate introduction to MARC coding for small- and medium-sized libraries. The final chapters of the guide (Chapters 13–14) are intended to bring all of the information together by providing some more practical guidelines for the implementation of a recon project, the introduction of MARC to your library, and editing MARC records derived from external sources.

Checklist:
Developing an Action Plan for Recon

Considerations

- Assign supervisory staff
- Establish written policies
- Produce detailed procedure manuals for staff
- Determine staffing requirements
- Determine training requirements and identify resources available
- Determine requirements for external services
- Establish timetable and task lists
- Allocate all necessary resources to the project
  - Money
  - Staff
  - Work location
  - Equipment and supplies

Further Reading

Carter, Ruth C., and Scott Bruntjen. *Data Conversion.* Professionaal Librarian Series. White Plains, NY: Knowledge Industry Publications, 1983.

Chiang, Belinda. *Retrospective Conversion through Carrollton Press: Manual of Procedures for Colgate University Libraries.* N.p.: Colgate University Library, 1983.

Collins, Jane D. "Planning for Retrospective Conversion." *Art Documentation* 1 (Summer 1982): 92-94.

Heitshu, Sara C., and Joan M. Quinn. "Serials Conversion at the University of Michigan." *Drexel Library Quarterly* 21 (Winter 1985): 62-76.

Petersen, Karla D. "Planning for Serials Retrospective Conversion." *Serials Review* 10 (Fall 1984): 73-78.

Purnell, Kathleen M. "Productivity in a Large-Scale Retrospective Conversion Project." In *Productivity in the Information Age: Proceedings of the 46th ASIS Annual Meeting 1983*, edited by Raymond F. Vondran, Anne Caputo, Carol Wasserman, and Richard A.V. Diener. White Plains, NY: Knowledge Industry Publications for American Society for Information Science, 1983.

Rearden, Phyllis, and John A. Whisler. "Retrospective Conversion at Eastern Illinois University." *Illinois Libraries* 65 (May 1983): 343-46.

Richardson, Valerie. "Retrospective Conversion Using LYNX and REMARC." *LASIE* 14 (September-October 1983): 14-25.

Rogers, Gloria H. "From Cards to Online: The Asian Connection." *Information Technology and Libraries* 5 (December 1986): 280-84.

Ryans, Cynthia C., and Margaret F. Soule. "Preparations for Retrospective Conversion: An Empirical Study." *Catholic Library World* 55 (December 1983): 221-23.

Wood, Susan. *Retrospective Conversion Procedure Manual for the Health Sciences Library.* Chapel Hill, NC: Health Sciences Library, University of North Carolina at Chapel Hill, 1984.

10
Machine-Readable Cataloging (MARC)

What is MARC?

MARC stands for MAchine-Readable Cataloging, and is a standard for the exchange of bibliographic information between automated library systems. It was initiated by the Library of Congress and has evolved into an international standard over the last twenty years. The American National Standards Institute (ANSI) is the organization for standards in the United States. An ANSI committee, Z39, was initially responsible for standardization in the field of library work, documentation, and related publishing practices. This Committee is now called the National Information Standards Organization (NISO). It is the 'library standards' organization in the United States, while the Canadian Standards Association (CSA) provides the same services in Canada, as does the British Standards Institution (BSI) in Great Britain. The international organization that coordinates much of the standards work in the information industry is the International Organization for Standardization (ISO), which is based in Geneva.

The basic structure of MARC is established through national and international standards and USMARC is a specific implementation of these standards. It is described in ANSI Z39.2-1979, *The American National Standard for Bibliographic Interchange on Magnetic Tape*. CANMARC, which contains some variations to USMARC in order to accommodate Canadian practices, also conforms to the international standard *Format for Bibliographic Information Interchange on Magnetic Tape* (ISO 2709-1973).

Throughout this section of the book, the term MARC will be used to indicate the generic name applied to the family of MARC formats, including USMARC, CANMARC, UKMARC, InterMARC etc. Specific differences between USMARC and CANMARC will be indicated where appropriate.

The Importance of MARC

The purpose of MARC is to provide a standard format for the *communication* of bibliographic information. Much has been written about the question of whether automated systems should be "MARC based." The important point about this question is that if communicating bibliographic information between systems or if resource sharing is important to the library then the selected system should be able to load MARC records from external sources and maintain that information in a format that permits the system to also generate MARC records from the library's database. In generating records for transfer to another system, the library programs must have retained all the essential information that is needed to recreate fields, subfields, and indicators.

From this description, it can be seen that the important concept of MARC is its function as a communications format. It does not matter if the library's system actually stores records in MARC format; indeed this may not be the most efficient way to access the records, but preservation of the information in a format that permits it to be recoded in MARC format is essential for exporting the records at some future date. The MARC format defines or delimits bibliographic information so that all types of library application programs can be applied to the library's database. For example, acquisitions, serials control, cataloging, circulation, and the public online catalog modules all manipulate portions of the record based on a common bibliographic format and appropriate additional information, such as vendors for acquisitions or patrons for circulation. The focus of this book is on using MARC to acquire the basic bibliographic information.

The use of MARC formats has become fundamental to the ability of libraries and bibliographic utilities to share and communicate bibliographic information. The importance of MARC is evident in the automation practices of many libraries today. MARC allows a library to:

Derive records. There are a number of sources, which are described in Appendix I, from which a library may obtain copies of standard cataloging in MARC format. If the library's automated system has a MARC interface then these derived records can be loaded into the local system and edited to suit the library's local practices and indicate the local holdings of the title. The ability to derive records in MARC format is important to economical recon projects, and for upgrading cataloging information from old card catalogs to current practices, and to take advantage of the added search capabilities that come with an online catalog. Derived MARC records can also be used on an ongoing basis for new cataloging.

Share cataloging. This is another aspect of deriving records. Use of the bibliographic utilities, such as OCLC, Utlas, and RLIN, or a shared regional system, means that a library can contribute its cataloging of unique items and derive other records that have been contributed by others in the network. MARC is the communications format that supports this kind of sharing and allows the library to send its records to the regional system, or build its records in the utility database and incorporate them into its local database.

Report to union catalogs. When a library has made an investment in automation and building a bibliographic database, the next logical step is to report new accessions to regional or national union catalogs in a machine-readable form, on either floppy diskettes or magnetic tape. The format for communicating these accessions should be MARC.

Compatibility with MARC and the ability to generate MARC records from a local biblio-graphic database is becoming fundamental to creating and maintaining union catalogs as more and more libraries automate.

Have flexibility. MARC provides libraries with flexibility. Having derived the basic record from a standard source such as a bibliographic utility or a CD-ROM product, the library can edit the record to suit its practices and add other information. The library can define fields for local use and rearrange existing ones without rekeying information and risking typographical errors. MARC increases the choices for manipulating bibliographic information in online systems, and provides a known structure for producing printed cata-logs and online public access from a single database of information.

The examples described above are all variations on the theme of cooperation and resource-sharing between libraries. MARC communications formats support the sharing of bibliographic information and provide small- and medium-sized libraries with an es-sential standard for obtaining quality cataloging in an economical manner and contribut-ing to resource sharing programs in their regions.

Before deciding whether to implement MARC in the library there are some disadvantages to using MARC which should be addressed. It is a complex standard which is far more detailed than a small or medium-sized library really needs. There are advantages to up-grading and improving bibliograpic information during the recon project by deriving MARC records but local storage of that information is expensive, as there are many sub-fields, tags, and indicators which the system may be unable to exploit. One of the purpos-es of this section of the book is to suggest a reasonable level of MARC coding which will provide the advantages of appropriately enhanced coding without the disadvantage of too costly storage and maintenance.

Not all libraries that are embarking on MARC coding will be loading their records into an automated system immediately. Many libraries are recognizing the use of MARC as an investment in the future and are presently producing card sets from MARC-based card production software. There is software available which permits the cataloger to create a MARC record, store that record for future use in an automated system, and create a card set for filing in the card catalog. Libraries are also using the CD-ROM-based MARC da-tabases to derive full MARC records for card sets and future automation uses.

The Elements of MARC

The Library of Congress has developed a variety of MARC record formats to accommo-date different types of cataloged materials. This has proved too complex for most small li-braries and in general the monographs format is used for all publications. While this may not be acceptable to the purists, it is practical for a small- or medium-sized library. This discussion of the use of MARC will focus on the monographs format. In addition to the monographs format, there are MARC formats defined for serials, maps, films, music, computer files, and archives and manuscripts. However, most small- and medium-sized libraries can accommodate their basic requirements within the monographs format.

At present, the standards committees are exploring the possibility of a single USMARC format. In an integrated format, fields would be used as appropriate to the item, not based on their material format. The formats have evolved over the past twenty years to support new types of materials and new forms of control. As the formats are separated from cataloging code, USMARC supports *AACR2* cataloging but does not restrict the user to that set of rules.

Each format consists of a number of elements, some of which are created by the library application software and some of which are created by the user. Some basic definitions were given in the introduction; these are now reviewed and other definitions are provided in the context of MARC formats. In order for the library application programs to process bibliographic information, and provide access, displays, and printed products from the database, the information must be loaded with a defined structure and then translated into the internal formats required by the specific library programs. The MARC format consists of the following elements.

Leader. The leader is fixed in length for all records and contains twenty-four characters. The leader contains information about the number of characters in the record and where fields begin and end in the record. This information is supplied by the system. The user provides information on the status of the record, the type of record, the bibliographic level, the encoding level (i.e., the degree of completeness of the bibliographic information), the descriptive cataloging form, and a code to indicate that linked records exist. In the majority of systems default values are supplied for these subfields and the user only changes them where appropriate. The leader allows a program to recognize a record and establish how it is to be processed.

Record directory. The directory is created by the MARC record-processing software. It contains one entry for each field in the record, showing the field label (tag), its length, and its starting position relative to the first field in the record. This allows the program to locate data in the record quickly and efficiently. The record directory is created and maintained by the software, and the user is not able to change the record directory. The importance of the record directory is that is allows the programs to handle the special complexities of bibliographic records—that is, variable length fields (e.g., a title field may vary in length from one character to over five hundred), and repeatable fields such as multiple authors or subjects, without having to set aside storage space in each record for the largest possible fields. Any length of field, the presence of a field, or no field can be indicated by the record directory without wasting storage space. Another benefit of the directory is that the program can efficiently locate specific fields, relative to the start of the record, without having to read the record sequentially until it finds the field that is required.

Control fields. The initial fields in a MARC record mostly contain fixed-length data elements and consist of a series of codes. Crawford (1984) points out that they are often called "fixed-length fields," but that this is misleading and incorrect. While the control fields may contain fixed-length data elements, control fields themselves are not inherently fixed-length. They differ from the variable-length fields in that they do not have indicators or subfields.

The most frequent use of these fields, some of which are derived from the bibliograpic description, is to provide the online retrieval software with easily accessible codes to characterize the item and allow the searcher to limit or qualify a search. For example, there are coded fields for country of publication, language, the type of material, and dates of publication. The individual control fields, all of which have tags beginning with "00," are discussed in the next chapter.

Variable length fields. The remaining fields of the record, whose tags begin with numerics other than "00," are variable data fields. The numeric tags of MARC have become very common as a method of identifying data for input or maintenance. Although the software may process numeric tags more efficiently and MARC defines tags in this way, there is no real reason why people should think, for example, of titles as being "245" fields when "TTL" would be intuitively more recognizable to the user. Many systems give the user a choice of prompts for data entry and when installing a system a choice may have to be made between numeric and mnemonic tags.

A tag is assigned to each independent element of a bibliographic record—for example, ISBN, personal author, uniform title, title, edition, imprint, etc. Each of the essential fields for a small- or medium-sized library is discussed in the next chapter.

Additional field content codes or designators are included in many of the variable fields to indicate to the processing programs other characteristics of the information in the field or its breakdown into subelements or subfields. The codes for characteristics of the fields are called indicators and each field can have at least two of these. Subfield delimiters indicate segments of the field, such as subtitle and the statement of responsibility in the title field "245."

Subfield Delimiters. The subfields, $a, $b, and $c, etc., delimit the various subsections of the record and are used in a variety of ways in the index-building process of an online catalog or database. For example, an index entry may be created from the "$a" subfield only, or combined"$a" and "$b" subfields.

The subfield delimiter precedes and identifies elements of the bibliographic record fields. Subfields are specified for each variable-length field in the record, but patterns are often repeated in related fields—for example, all types of subject headings, or for personal name main and added entries. In most MARC fields, subfield delimiters are lower-case alphabetic characters preceded by a special character. This special character varies with different MARC-based systems, but is often one of: $, l, ↑,‡ or ▼. This book uses the "$" followed by the appropriate lower-case alphabetic or numeric character to indicate the subfield delimiter.

The application software will also insert two other delimiters which are necessary to label the parts of a record. These are the field terminator and record terminator. These indicate to the program when the end of a field or record has been reached and their positions correspond to the information at the beginning of the record about the lengths of fields and the length of the whole record. These are solely for the use of the application programs and do not have to be managed by the operator.

Indicators. Many of the variable-length fields in the MARC record also contain one or two indicators. These have different values depending on the field they are associated with, but their purpose is to act as triggers to the library programs regarding some characteristic of the information in the field, such as its source, and/or how the program should treat the information. Examples of indicators, and all the other database features described here, are given in Chapters 11 through 12. If the indicators are not defined for a particular field then the spaces are left blank by the operator or cataloger.

Some automated system manuals provide default values for the indicators, since the source of information may not be obvious when working from old shelf-list cards or the actual book. Chapter 13, which discusses the implementation of MARC coding in a library, addresses the question of which indicators are essential to the integrity and accuracy of the library's database.

The following example illustrates some of the features discussed here:

245 1 4 $aThe computer entrepreneurs :$bwho's making it big and how in America's
              upstart industry /$cby Robert Levering, Michael Katz, and Milton Moskowit.

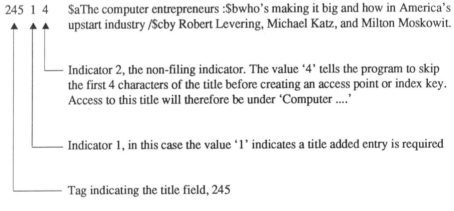

Indicator 2, the non-filing indicator. The value '4' tells the program to skip the first 4 characters of the title before creating an access point or index key. Access to this title will therefore be under 'Computer ....'

Indicator 1, in this case the value '1' indicates a title added entry is required

Tag indicating the title field, 245

Each field and subfield that a small- or medium-sized library might use is described in detail in the next chapter. The indicators and subfields for each field are also discussed, along with the field-by-field description of a bibliographic record.

Checklist:
Machine-Readable Cataloging (MARC)

The Importance of MARC

- deriving records
- shared cataloging
- reporting to union catalogs
- flexibility for development and automation

The Elements of MARC

- leader
- record directory
- control fields
- variable length fields
- subfield delimiters
- indicators

Further Reading

American National Standards Institute. *American National Standard for Bibliographic Information Interchange on Magnetic Tape.* New York: ANSI, 1979.

Attig, John C. "The Concept of a MARC Format." *Information Technology and Libraries* 2 (March 1983): 7-17.

———. "US/MARC Formats: Underlying Principles." *Library of Congress Information Bulletin* 41 (April 23, 1982): 120-24.

British Standards Institution. *Bibliographic Information Interchange Format for Magnetic Tape.* London: BSI, 1971.

Crawford, W. *MARC for Library Use: Understanding the USMARC Formats.* White Plains, NY: Knowledge Industry Publications, 1984.

Library of Congress. Automated Systems Office. *MARC Formats for Bibliographic Data.* Washington, DC: Library of Congress, 1980- . Looseleaf.

Library of Congress. Automation Planning and Liaison Office. *Authorities: A MARC Format.* Washington, DC: Library of Congress, 1981.

Library of Congress. Network Development and MARC Standards Office. *USMARC Authority Format Including Guidelines for Content Designation.* Washington, DC: Library of Congress, 1987- . Loosleaf. (Superintendent of Documents No. LC1.6/4:Au8)

———. *USMARC Specifications for Record Structure, Character Sets, Tapes.* Washington, DC: Library of Congress, 1987.

McDonald, David R. "MARC: the Foundation of Library Automation." *Journal of Academic Librarianship* 13 (July 1987): 168c-168d : insert between 168-69.

National Library of Canada. *Canadian MARC Communication Format: Mini-MARC.* Ottawa: National Library of Canada, 1982.

————. *Canadian MARC Communication Format: Minimal Level.* Ottawa: National Library of Canada, 1987.

————. Canadian MARC Office. *Canadian MARC Communications Format: Bibliographic Data.* Ottawa: National Library of Canada, 1988- . Looseleaf. (DSS cat. no. SN214/1988E)

————. Canadian MARC Office. *Canadian MARC Communications Format: Authorities.* 3rd. Edition. Ottawa: National Library of Canada, 1988- . Looseleaf. (DSS cat. no. SN3-123/1988E)

Simmons, Peter, and Alan Hopkinson. *CCF: The Common Communications Format.* Paris: Unesco For The General Information Programme and UNISIST, 1984.

Wiggins, Beacher. "The Processing and Distribution of International MARC Data by the Library of Congress." *International Leads* 2 (Spring 1988): 7.

11
MARC Bibliographic Records

This chapter provides a detailed, field-by-field guide to the various sections of the MARC bibliographic format. The level of coding discussed in this chapter is appropriate to the types of system being selected by small- and medium-sized libraries today. Monographs and serials format fields are described and the differences between the formats are indicated where appropriate. It is likely that your system will accommodate most of the basic fields discussed in this chapter.

In reviewing these fields, the user may recognize some anachronisms that are included in the MARC formats, because one of the purposes of the formats was for card production. Thus main and added entries are differentiated; however, in the online environment the concept of main entry carries much less weight. Typically the online indexes, such as the author index, will contain both the main and added entries without differentiating between them.

It is important to note that the following is not a comprehensive list of MARC fields or subfields. All elements described below have been selected based on their suitability for small and medium-sized libraries, the level of detail that is normally required for a catalog in this kind of library, and the types of automated library systems likely to be selected. Users who require greater detail are referred to the official MARC manuals cited at the end of this chapter. Most of the examples given in this chapter have been extracted from one or other of the official MARC manuals.

Components of the MARC Record

Leader

The leader segment of a MARC record provides information to the application program about how to process the record. The leader, which is the first twenty-four characters of the record, is created by the program at the time the record is created or changed. The most important element of it, as far as the library is concerned, is the record status. For those libraries that load records from an external source, the record status indicates whether the record is a new or changed one. Based on the record status, the program either adds a record and creates the necessary searching access points, or looks for an existing record and replaces it with the changed record. In the case of changed records local information, such as local call number and holdings, must be preserved and linked to the changed bibliographic record. "Deleted" is the third permissible record status. A record with this status will no longer be displayed when a user is searching the online catalog, since it presumably represents a title that is no longer in the library collection. Deleting records and assigning this status will be a function that is controlled by the catalogers through the cataloging module.

The leader has a fixed length of twenty-four characters. The first five characters are created by the processing program.

Character
Position

0-4 Logical record length, i.e. the number of characters in the record

The next 3 characters are used as follows:

5 Record status

    n   - New record
    c   - Corrected or revised record
    d   - Deleted record

6 Type of record

    a   - Language material, printed or microform

7 Bibliographic level (monographs format)

    m   - Monographs

    Bibliographic level (serials format)

    b   - Component part, serial
    s   - Serial

Most of the rest of the leader is created by the program processing the record and tells other programs how the record is laid out and how many elements and fields it contains.

The exceptions are character positions 17 and 18, which are coded by the user as follows:

17   Encoding level

ᵇ   Full level[1]
1   Sublevel 1 (material not examined)
5   Sublevel 5 (partial preliminary record)
7   Sublevel 7 (minimal level record)
8   Sublevel 8 (pre-publication record)
z   Sublevel z (not applicable, signifies that the concept of encoding level does not apply)

The library should accept the coding supplied with derived records, or assign one appropriate to its level of MARC coding, for example 7-minimal level record.

18   Descriptive cataloging form

ᵇ   Record does not follow ISBD conventions
a   Record is AACR2
i   Record is in ISBD format

Unless this information is supplied in a derived record, in recon use blank as the default value for position 18 of the leader.

The Directory

The directory contains more detailed information about the layout of the record. It is created and managed by the application software and, like the leader, will not be seen by the users during normal operations. The purpose of the directory is to provide a way for programs to identify and retrieve segments of the records quickly and efficiently. The format of the directory is part of the MARC standard, and as such means that programs which understand this format can process records from a variety of sources without major structural changes. Only programmers and systems analysts need to look at and analyze record directories, and most often they are doing so in development or problem-solving situations.

Variable-Length Control Fields

The variable control fields contain data which may be required for processing the bibliographic record. There are no indicators or subfields in this segment of the record and each piece of data begins in a fixed location relative to the first character position in the field. These fields are not repeatable.

---

[1]Throughout chapters 12 and 13 the symbol ᵇ is used to indicate a required blank space.

001 Control Number (Record identification number). This field is provided in all MARC records and must be unique to the system that originates the record. Field 001 does not have a fixed length or pattern. It contains the library's own control number and will usually be generated automatically by the application software the first time the record is created and saved.

005 Date and Time of Latest Transaction. The date and time provide important information for processing the record and are used to verify updates and changes to the catalog. These elements are generally assigned by the application program and changed each time the record is modified and refiled.

007 Physical Description Fixed Field. If the recon project includes records for microforms or audio/visual materials then some of the subfields in this field should be completed. This field is not required for other language material records. The field consists of thirteen character positions (00-12), but only the first two need to be completed for the level of coding we are discussing in this book.

For microforms the following coding would be appropriate:

Character
Position

00   General Materials Designation

    h   - Microform

Other codes in this subfield are for materials such as maps, globes, sound recordings, graphics, motion pictures, and videorecordings. The detailed coding for these materials is beyond the scope of this book. The MARC manuals referenced at the end of this chapter will provide the necessary information if required.

01   Specific Material Designation

    a   - Aperture card
    b   - Microfilm cartridge
    c   - Microfilm cassette
    d   - Microfilm reel
    e   - Microfiche
    f   - Microfiche cassette
    g   - Microopaque
    z   - Other

Example   Leader - position 6   a
            Leader - position 7   s

            007   hd-----------

This coding would be appropriate for periodical language materials, such as the microfilm versions of the *New York Times, Washington Post,* or the *Globe and Mail.*

For audio/visual materials the following coding would be appropriate:

Character
Position

00 General Materials Designation

m - Motion picture
v - Videorecording

01 Specific Material Designation

Motion Picture

r - Film reeel
z - Other

Videorecording

f - Videocassete
z - Other

Example   Leader - position 6   a
           Leader - position 7   m

           007   vf-----------

This coding would be appropriate for a videocassette of *Gone with the Wind.*

008 Fixed-Length Data Elements - General information. The fixed-length data elements are a group of approximately twenty elements (depending on the version of MARC being used) which all have specific and unchanging positions in the field 008. The total length of field 008 is forty characters (counted from 00 to 39), but not all of these have to be used if the library is entering a minimal level of MARC coding. The elements listed here are probably the most important ones, and the ones that can generally be derived from a catalog card if the recon is being done directly from the shelf-list cards. Data elements that are not used should be left blank.

A MARC-based cataloging system should not require the operator to count positions when entering data in this field, as early versions of CD-ROM systems did. Typically, the system will prompt the operator with understandable mnemonics for the elements, and then store the information in the appropriate positions.

The purpose of the 008 fields is to provide some basic information and codes about the bibliographic descrition. These codes are often used to select records for printed products— for example, selecting by date of publication, language, or country of publication. In an online catalog they are used to qualify searches, and thus narrow the results. For example, after searching for all titles relating to a subject, the patron might decide that she only wanted to see recently published titles and limit the search to post-1986 titles. In order to filter these titles from an existing hit list, the system would check the date elements in the 008 field since they are in a fixed position and can be found more quickly than from the imprint field, which is variable field 260.

Differences between the use of 008 elements in the monographs and serials formats are indicated below.

Character
Position

0-5   Date entered on file

           This is usually generated by the system and does not change when the record
           is subsequently edited or deleted. The format of the date is metric, that is,
           "yymmdd."

           Example: 720405 means April 5, 1972

6   Type of publication date code (monographs format)

           This subfield is used to describe the types of dates found in the two following
           subfields: Date 1 and Date 2. For example, a single-volume monograph
           would normally only have one date, entered in Date 1 and an 's' in position 6
           would indicate that there was no need to check Date 2. However, if the mon-
           ograph were a multivolume work published over several years the code
           would be 'm' and Date 1 would contain the date of publication of the first
           volume and Date 2 the date of the last volume.

           c   - Two dates, date of publication and copyright date
           m   - Multiple dates or open-ended date
           n   - Unknown date of publication
           r   - Two dates, reprint/re-issue and original
           s   - Single known date

           In the monographs format codes 'c', 'm' and 'r' are only used if Date 1 and
           Date 2 are being used (see examples below).

Publication status code (serials format)

The use of this subfield is different if you are cataloging a serial publication. In this case 'c' indicates that the title is still being published and therefore there will only be a starting date in Date 1. If the title has ceased publication the starting date will be in positions 7-10 and the closing date in positions 11-14, with the code 'd' in position 6. If the title is still being published Date 2, positions 11-14, is given the value '9999'.

c   - currently published
d   - dead
u   - status unknown

7-10   Date 1 (mongraphs format)

Beginning date of publication (serials format)

This element is 4 characters long, and the year of publication should be used, e.g., 1895, 1987, etc.

11-14   Date 2

Second date (monographs format)

In the same format as Date 1, this element is used for the second date when a publication is issued over a period of two or more years. The type of publication date code corresponding to use of Date 2 is "m" (multiple or open-ended date). Date 2 equal to '9999' indicates that the multi-volume work is not yet completed. Date 2 is not used when type of publication date code = "s", (single known date).

Examples (monographs format)

Imprint date	Code	Date 1	Date 2
1966	s	1966	ƀƀƀƀ
[1969?]	s	1969	ƀƀƀƀ
1966 [c1965]	c	1966	1965
1966-1967	m	1966	1967
1966-	m	1966	9999
[n.d.]	n	ƀƀƀƀ	ƀƀƀƀ
1966 [c1950]	r	1966	1741

In the last example, Date 2 has the value '1741' because the title was originally published in Dublin in 1741.

Ending date of publication (serials format)

This element has four numeric characters representing the ending date of publication for the serial title being cataloged. If the title is currently published and continuing the value '9999' is entered in Date 2.

Examples (serials format)

Code	Beginning date	Ending date
c	1967	9999
d	1960	1971
u	1970	9999

The first example represents a continuing serial that began in 1967. In the last example the starting date was estimated to the nearest decade and the code 'u' was used to indicate that the real status of the date is unknown.

15-17   Country of publication code

The MARC manuals contain a comprehensive table of codes to be used in this element. The codes can be up to three characters in length, and generally indicate only the country of publication. The exception to this is the codes for the United States, Canada, Australia, United Kingdom, China and the U.S.S.R. which breakdown the coding for States, Provinces, or other political sub-units. For these countries the codes use the first two characters to represent a state, province or other subdivision and the third character position to indicate the larger entity.

The country of publication codes are standard for USMARC and CANMARC and are reproduced in their respective MARC manuals as well as in user manuals for specific automated systems.

Some examples of the expanded codes are:

us	United States
ndu	North Dakota
cn	Canada
onc	Ontario
uk	United Kingdom
stk	Scotland
ur	U.S.S.R.
unr	Ukraine
err	Estonia

Examples of other countries are:

at	Australia
cl	Chile
fr	France
sp	Spain

It is important to use the correct codes for each country as provided in the MARC manuals.

18   Frequency (serials format)

Used when cataloging serials and corresponds to the frequency information in field 310 (see below). Some of the most commonly used codes for this element are:

b̸	- irregular
a	- annual
d	- daily
m	- monthly
q	- quarterly
w	- weekly
u	- unknown
z	- other frequencies
n	- not applicable, not a serial

22   Intellectual Level Code

Used to indicate the level of juvenile books.

blank	- not applicable
j	- Juvenile work
u	- School textbooks (at first level)
v	- School textbooks (at second level)

23   Form of Reproduction Code

This code is used to indicate if the work has been produced in a size too small to be read by the human eye. It is also used to indicate reproduction in some other medium, such as Braille or large print.

a	- Microfilm
b	- Microfiche
c	- Micoropaque
d	- Large print
f	- Braille

g	- Punched paper tape
h	- Magnetic tape
i	- Multimedia
r	- Regular print
z	- Other form of reproduction
ʬ	- Not a reproduction

33   Fiction indicator

This code differs in USMARC and CANMARC. For USMARC the codes are:

0	Not fiction
1	Fiction

For CANMARC:

Literary Text and Type of Publication Indicator

c	Comic strip
d	Drama (including television plays, scenarios, etc)
e	Essays (belles lettres)
f	Fiction
h	Humour, satire, etc.
i	Letters (as a literary form)
j	Short stories
m	Miscellaneous information
p	Poetry (including non-literary works in verse)
s	Speeches, oratory
ʬ	Non-fiction

35-37   Language Code

As with the country of publication codes there is an established list of codes which should be used when created original MARC records. This code is used to indicate the predominant language of the work.

Some frequently used examples include:

eng	English
fre	French
ger	German
hun	Hungarian
ita	Italian
mul	multilingual

rus   Russian

spa   Spanish

The elements described here are the most important ones for small- and medium-sized libraries. The other elements that are not described here can be left blank. For examples of field 008 refer to the records reproduced at the end of this chapter.

Variable-Length Fields (010-899)

The remaining part of the record consists of a variable number of variable-length fields. As described in the introduction to this section of the book, it is this part of the MARC record that contains the information we are familiar with from a catalog card.

Fields in this part of the record are grouped in "levels." For example the 100–130 fields contain the main entry and are known as the 100 level or 1XX fields. Similarly, subject entries are the 600 level or 6XX fields.

Theoretically, all variable fields can be repeated as many times as necessary to accommodate multiple ISBNs, authors, subjects, etc. In practice the nature of cataloging is such that many fields are not repeatable. An example of this is the main entry fields in the 100 level segment of the record. There can only be one main entry. Repeatable fields and subfields are noted in the following pages by an 'R'. The absence of an 'R' indicates the element is not repeatable and can only occur once in the record.

In this section of the book, each field is described as follows:

Field tag number   The numeric tag which defines the content of the field, e.g., 100 for a Main Entry - Personal Name.

R   If applicable, the character 'R' indicates that this field may be repeated if required. For example, 600, Subject Entry - Personal Name would be repeatable so that a book about more than one person could be given appropriate subject entries.

Field name   The official name of the field which corresponds to the field tag number stored in the database.

Then, there is a brief description of how this field is used, followed by information on:

Subfields   A list of the important subfields for the level of coding that is being described in this manual. If an individual subfield is repeatable within the field, there is an 'R' after the subfield label. For example, the subfield for each subordinate unit in the heirarchy of an organization for a corporate author entry is repeatable. (See field 110)

Indicators

For fields where indicators are defined, indicators 1 and 2 are shown. Default values, which can be used if the correct value is not obvious from the work in hand, or from the shelf-list card in a recon, are shown by <u>underlining</u>. These default values are suggestions of the authors, based on usage in automated library systems, not officially sanctioned by the source agencies, Library of Congress and National Library of Canada.

Examples

For each field described here a number of examples are provided. Most of these examples are extracted from the Library of Congress or National Library of Canada MARC manuals. Punctuation, spacing, and the order of elements has been carefully laid out and may be used as a guide. However, punctuation does vary with different systems and utilities so you should check you own system manuals as well. Where appropriate the rules for the description of library materials in the General International Standard Bibliographic Description (ISBD(G)) have been used and examples have been selected from the USMARC and CANMARC manuals.

Tag numbers are not repeated in these examples but the indicators and subfield labels are all included.

If a blank space is important to the layout of the field, and not obvious from the sense of the field content, it is indicated by ƀ

010 Library of Congress Card Number (LCCN). An eight-digit number, preceded by three blanks or an alphabetic prefix. Occasionally the LCCN is followed by alphabetic or alphanumeric characters. These should be included. The numeric portion needs to be expanded if the number on the card or in the book does not contain eight digits. To expand the number to eight digits insert zeros (0) after the first two digits until the required number is reached. Hyphens should be dropped.

Subfields

$a
LC card number

Indicators

Blank

Examples

$aƀƀƀ80028345
$aƀƀƀ79000234
$aƀƀƀ82144414

$aʋʋʋ65077628ʋMN
$anuc80233224

In the first example the original card number would have been 80-28345, similarly 79-234 becomes 79000234, and 82-144414 is entered 82144414. The final example is a National Union Catalog record.

016   National Library of Canada Bibliographic Control Number (CANMARC only). Similar to the LC card number, this is a nine-digit number, which needs to be expanded if the number on the card or in the book does not contain nine digits. To expand the number to nine digits insert zeros (0) after the first two digits until the required number is reached. All hyphens should be dropped.

Subfields $a   NLC bibliographic record number (field 001 in Canadiana
                                 records distributed through NLC's MARC Record
                                 Distribution Service)

Indicators   Blank

Examples $a 740038109
                     $a 860913910
                     $a 850995302

In the first example the original card number was C74-3810-9, the second was C86-91391-0, and the third C85-099530-2.

020   R   International Standard Book Number (ISBN). This ten-digit number is increasingly becoming the unique number by which books and their corresponding MARC records are identified. It is an international number assigned by the publisher from blocks assigned by national agencies. The final digit, which is a check-digit used to check the validity of the number, may be an 'X'. If the number does not have ten digits, and it is published in the United States, Great Britain, Canada (English language only), Australia, or New Zealand, insert a zero (0) in front of the number.

Subfields $a   ISBN
                                  $c   Terms of availability (price)

Indicators   Blank

Examples $a0416866808 (pbk) :$c$2.95
                                  $a0471085693 :$c$55.00 (est.)

If the library owns both the hardback and paperback copies of a title and wishes to record both ISBN numbers in the same MARC record, this field can be repeated.

035   R   Local System Control Number. There are a variety of ways to use this field. It is most often used by libraries who derive records from a bibliographic utility to retain the record number from the utility database. Users of OCLC, WLN, or Utlas should all consider this application for the 035 field. Generally the MARC loading program for the library's automated system can be directed to load that number in this field. Other libraries use 035 for an accession number or record number from an old system, if one of these has a significance that needs to be retained in the automated environment.

Subfields	$a	Local system control number

Indicators	Blank

There is no prescribed format for the content of this field.

040   Cataloging Source. This field is used to indicate the source of the cataloging, typically Library of Congress, National Library of Medicine, National Library of Canada, etc. If the library is cataloging the title originally, with no derived cataloging, then the library's inter-library loan symbol should be entered.

Subfields	$a	Original cataloging agency code

Indicators	Blank

Examples	$aDLC
	$aDNLM
	$aCaOONL
	$aCaOTU
	$aBNB

These symbols represent Library of Congress, National Library of Medicine, National Library of Canada, University of Toronto, and British National Bibliography respectively. The library should maintain its own set of acceptable codes for this field, including the national codes plus any local codes. If element 39 of the 008 field is blank, this field should also be left blank.

050   R   Library of Congress Call Number. Only call numbers actually assigned by LC should be placed in this field. It is not used to record the call number that the library assigns to the title in its collection, even if it is identical to the one assigned by LC. Call numbers for the library's own collection are recorded in the local holdings field described at the end of this section.

Subfields	$a	R	·	LC classification number
/	$b			Book number / Cutter number

Indicators	1	Existence in the LC Collection

ɰ - information not provided
0   - in LC
1   - Not in LC

2   Source of Classification/Call Number
     ɰ   - no information provided
     1   - assigned by LC
     4   - assigned by agency other than LC

Note: CANMARC does not define the second indicator, and hence it should be left blank when using the CANMARC format.

Example   01 $aE302.6.B9$bL7 1979

For a book about Aaron Burr, United States President, by Milton Lomask, in the LC collection with a call number assigned by LC. In general this field will be used as a source of call numbers for the library deriving a MARC record. This field will not be used by libraries who are creating original MARC records.

082   R   Dewey Decimal Classification Number. Similar to field 050, and used in the same way, this one is for Dewey Decimal Classification Numbers.

Subfields $a   R   Dewey number
            $2   Source (i.e. Dewey edition number)

Indicators 1   Type of edition

                  blank - no edition information recorded
                  0   - Full edition of Dewey
                  1   - Abridged edition
                  2   - Abridged NST version

            2   Source of DDC number

                  blank - no information provided
                  1   - assigned in LC
                  4   - assigned by agency other than LC

Note: CANMARC does not define the second indicator; it should be left blank.

Example   01 $a973.4/6/0924$219

For the same book about Aaron Burr, used in 050 field example, with the number assigned from the 19th edition of DDC. In many instances the Dewey number is divided into as many as three segments by the '/' [slash] sign to allow libraries to cut long numbers without assigning professional cataloging talent to the task. Like the LC call number field, this field is used as a source of Dewey numbers by libraries deriving cataloging information.

Main Entries (100 Level)

The next group of fields are for author main entries, and are often known as the '1XX' or 100 level fields. If the book being cataloged has a title main entry (other than uniform title main entry), then there is no 1XX field. By definition of cataloging conventions, there can only be one 1XX field in each record, whereas many other fields can be repeated as many times as appropriate. Substitutes, such as editors or illustrators, should not be entered here. There are many subfields in most of these fields; however, bearing in mind the intended audience for this handbook, only the essential and frequently used subfields are described.

A number of subfields are the same in each field of the 100 level, regardless of context. These include:

$a   Name
$e   Relator (the relationship between the name and the material being described, e.g., editor, illustrator)
$k   Form subheading (a number of standardized phrases, such as 'Laws, statutes, etc.')
$t   Title (of a work)

100   Main Entry Heading - Personal Name. Used for personal names as the main entry.

Subfields	$a		Name (surnames and forenames)
	$q		Expansion of initials in parenthesis, i.e., a qualification of the name in fuller form
	$b		Number (roman numerals)
	$c	R	Titles or other words associated with name
	$d		Date

Indicators	1	Type of personal name
	0	- Forename only
	1	- Single surname
	2	- Multiple surname
	3	- Name of the family

	2	Specifies whether the main entry is also the subject of the work

| | | 0 | - Main entry / subject relationship irrelevant |
| | | 1 | - Main entry is the subject |

Examples	10	$aRichards, W. G.$q(William Graham)
	10	$aGroulx, Lionel Adolphe,$d1878-1967.
	1∅	$aIrwin, Hadley.
	10	$aBrown, Alford Eugene,$d1897-$ecomp.
	20	$aRiano y Montero, Juan Facundo,$d1828-1901.
	20	$aMendelssohn-Bartholdy, Felix.
	11	$aIacocca, Lee.
	01	$aJohn the Baptist.

110 Main Entry Heading - Corporate Name. Enter in this field any corporate name which represents the main entry of the work.

Subfields	$a		Name
	$b	R	Subheading (each subordinate unit in the heirarchy of the organization)
	$d	R	Date
	$c		Place
	$k		Form subheading

Indicators	1	Type of corporate name

		0	- Surname (inverted)
		1	- Place or place and name
		2	<u>- Name (direct order)</u>

	2	Specifies whether the main entry is also the subject of the work

| | | 0 | - Main entry / subject relationship irrelevant |
| | | 1 | - Main entry is the subject |

Examples	20	$aAutomobile Association (Great Britain).$bPublications Division.
	20	$aAmerican Association of Critical-Care Nurses.
	10	$aUnited States.$kTreaties, etc.

111 Main Entry Heading - Conference or Meeting. This field is used if the name of a conference or meeting is the main entry of the work. It is most commonly used for the proceedings of a conference.

Subfields	$a	Name of meeting or place element
	$q	Name if entry element ($a) under place

	$d	Date
	$c	Place
	$n	Number or designation

Indicators   1   Type of conference of meeting

0   - Surname (inverted)
1   - Place or place and name
2   <u>- Name (direct order)</u>

2   Specifies whether the main entry is also the subject of the work

0   - Main entry / subject relationship irrelevant
1   - Main entry is the subject

Examples   20 $aVatican Council$n(1st :$d1869-1870)
20   $aNational Conference on Artificial Intelligence$d(1982
:$cCarnegie-Mellon University and University of Pittsburgh)

130   Main Entry Heading - Uniform Title

Uniform title main entries occur very seldom. The title occurs in the author area of the card but looks like a title. It is used for works which appear under varying titles which have no corresponding personal or corporate author main entry. An example of this use of a uniform title is the Bible. The uniform title field, in the title level of the record (240), is used if either 100 or 110 has been used for the main entry.

Subfields $a   Uniform title heading
$p   Part or section
$t   Title of the work
$k   Form subheading

Indicators   1   Non-filing characters

0-9   - Number of characters ignored in filing

2   Specifies whether the main entry is also the subject of the work

0   - Main entry / subject relationship irrelevant
1   - Main entry is the subject

Examples   00 $aBible.$kSelections.
            00    $aBible.$pN.T.
            00    $aDead Sea Scrolls.
            00    $aChanson de Roland.

Title/Imprint Entries (200 Level)

The next section of the record contains the 2XX or 200 level fields and contains title and imprint information. In most systems the 245, which is the title field, is required and must be completed before any record can be filed. This group of fields make use of a very important indicator—the nonfiling indicator. The value for this indicator, which can vary from 0 to 9, is used to tell the processing program how many characters to skip before creating a search or index entry point. For example, the title *The Friendship notebook : a personal journal* would have a value '4' in the second indicator position. This would tell the program that four characters, THEḄ, must be skipped, and the search access word is "Friendship." Some other examples of nonfiling indicator values are:

Leading article	Value of nonfiling indicator
A	2
An	3
Le	3
L'	2
Les	4

In the 2XX title fields, the nonfiling indicator is always the second one. However, the MARC formats are not always inherently consistent and the added titles entries in the 7XX section of the record use the first indicator as the nonfiling indicator. Whether you are deriving records or creating original ones, it is important to check these indicators very carefully, since successful retrieval of the title depends on correct creation of the index entry point.

240 Uniform Title. A uniform title usually appears in square brackets ([]) below the main entry. It is used to bring together works which may have been published under a variety of titles. Note that the way the indicators are used is different to a main entry uniform title.

Subfields	$a		Uniform title
	$p	R	Part of section

Indicators	1	Uniform title on LC printed card/added entries
	0	- Not printed on cards
	1	- Printed on cards

	2	Non-filing characters
	0-9	- Number of characters ignored in filing
Example	10	$aDeclaration of Independence.

In this example, for the Declaration of Independence, the 110 field would have contained "United States" as the main entry of work and field 245 might have contained *Declaration of the Independence of the United States.*

245 Title Statement. The title field is often the only field that is required, or mandatory, in the creation of an online bibliographic record. Thus the library application software, or recon software, will allow you to create brief records with little more than a title and a date if you do not have the full information about the book immediately available. On a catalog card the title statement appears directly below the author, or if there is no author, on the first line. The title statement is divided into a number of subfields which are described below. The punctuation used in these examples is based on the International Standard Bibliographic Description (ISBD), which has been incorporated into the *Anglo-American Cataloguing Rules*, Second Edition (*AACR2*).

Title	The title proper consists of all text up to and including the colon (or semi-colon on older cards). The title proper information is placed in the $a subfield of the 245 field and ends with [space][colon], i.e., ' :' if there is other title information in subfield $b, or '.' [period] if there is no other title information and no statement of responsibility. If there is just a statement of responsibility then the title proper ends with ' /' [space][forward slash].
Other title information	This subfield contains other title information appearing after the colon or semi-colon and continues up to and including the forward slash (/), or on older cards, the period or comma. This information is placed in the $b subfield, ending with [space][forward slash], i.e., ' /' to indicate a statement of responsibility follows, or '.' [period], if there is no statement of responsibility.
Statement of responsibility	The statement of responsibility repeats the author statement from the title page and may include the joint authors, illustrators, and editors, etc. Some older cards do not include a statement of responsibility, in which case this subfield can be omitted. The statement is placed in the $c subfield and should end with a period.
Subfields $a	Short title/title proper
$b	Subtitle or remainder of title
$c	Remainder of title area transcription, e.g., statement of responsibility

Indicators	1	Title added entry

		0	- No title added entry
		1	- Title added entry

	2	Non-filing characters

		0-9	- Number of characters ignored in filing

Example	10	$aAcross the city line :$ba white community in transition / $cRobert B. Zehner, F. Stuart Chapin, Jr., in collaboration with Joseph T. Howell.
	04	$aThe Addison-Wesley manual of nursing practice /$cDolores F. Saxton ... [et al.]
	00	$aJournal of biosocial science.

The remainder of the 2XX fields relate to edition statements and the imprint.

250 Edition Statement. If there is an edition statement on the card or the book, this is included in field 250.

Subfields	$a	Edition
	$b	Remainder of edition statement

Indicators	Blank

Example	$a4th ed.
	$aRevised /$bby John Smith.

260 Imprint / Release. The place of publication, publisher, and date(s) of publication are entered in this field. The place of publication is entered in the $a subfield, which may be repeated if the publication was published simultaneously in more than one place. This subfield ends with [space][colon], i.e., ' :', or [colon], ';' in the first $a subfield if there is a second $a subfield. The $b subfield contains the publisher name and may also be repeated if more than one publisher is involved. End this subfield with a [comma] and no spaces. The date is placed in the $c subfield and 'c' should be included if the date is derived from the copyright date.

Subfields	$a	R	Place of publication distribution etc.
	$b	R	Name of publisher, distributor etc.
	$c	R	Date of publication, distribution etc.

Indicators   1   Presence of publisher in imprint

<u>0 -</u>   <u>Publisher, distributor statement is present</u>
1 -   Publisher, distributor etc. statement is absent

                2   blank (Monographs format)

                2   Relationship between publisher and added entry (Serials format)

<u>0 -</u>   <u>Publisher, distributor etc. is not the same as the issuing</u>
       <u>body transcribed in the added entry</u>
1 -   Publisher, distributor etc. is the same as the issuing
       body transcribed in the added entry

Examples   0ʖ $aLondon :$bWeidenfeld and Nicholson,$c1987.
            0ʖ $aNew York ;$aChichester :$bWiley,$cc1981.
            1ʖ $c1984.

Leave the second indicator blank if there is no added entry that relates to the publisher or issuing body of a serial.

263 Projected Publication Date. This field will not be used if you are creating a record with the work in hand. However, you will often see it in derived records where the cataloging copy has been created for Cataloging in Publication (CIP). It may be used in creating an original record if it is a pre-order record. Derived records with this field should be checked carefully to ensure the descriptive cataloging matches the actual publication. The format of the date in subfield $a is 'yymm'.

Subfield $a   Projected publication date

Indicators   Blank

Examples $a7812
              $a80--

In the first example the projected date was December 1978, in the second the month is unknown but the publication was projected for 1980.

Physical Description (300 Level)

300 R Collation. This is the information that is traditionally found on the line below the imprint and indented two spaces. It describes the physical format of the item being cataloged. Four subfields are listed below but many libraries simplify this information and place it all in the $a subfield.

Subfields	$a	R	Extent of item
	$b		Other physical details
	$c	R	Dimensions
	$e		Accompanying material ($d in CANMARC)

Indicators   Blank

Examples $a2 v. (2004 p. in various pagings) :$bill., forms ;$c25cm
              $a1 v.   [simplified version indicating 1 volume]
              $axix, 289 p. :$bill. ;$c25cm.

The remaining two fields that are described in the 300 level of the record are used when cataloging serials in order to record the bibliographic information relating to frequency of publication and the publishing history of the title in terms of the volumes issued and the dates of publication. If the title is still being published, then the starting date and volume are recorded and it is left as an open entry.

310 Current frequency [serials format].

Subfields $a   Current frequency

Indicators   Blank

Example $a   Quarterly

362 R Dates of Publication and Volume Designations [Serials Format]. This field is used when cataloging serials to record the actual publishing dates and volume designations during the life of a title. It should not be used for local holdings. These are entered in field 850.

Subfields $a   Volume and date designations

Indicators   1   Format of the date

                         0 - Formatted style
                         1 - Unformatted note

               2   Blank

Examples   0ɓ $aVol. 1 (1967)-v.4 (1971)
               0ɓ $aVol. 1, no. 1 (Jan./Mar. 1974)-
               1ɓ $aBegan in 1948.

Series Entries (400 Level)

In assigning the series fields a distinction is made between series that are traced in the same way as they are found in the series statement (440), and those that are traced differently or not at all (490).

With the introduction of *AACR2* the practice of author/title series tracings was discontinued. This means that newer records will use only fields 440 and 490 for traced titles, and untraced or differently traced series respectively. Older records derived from external sources will still use fields 400, 410, and 411. Editing of these fields will depend on your library's policy for the use of *AACR2*.

440   R   Series Statement - Title (Traced). This field is used for series that are traced in the form that is found on the title page or elsewhere in the book.

Subfields	$a	Title
	$v	Volume or number
Indicators	1	Blank
	2	Non-filing characters
	0-9	- Number of characters ignored in filing
Examples	⩾0	$aBooks for professionals
	⩾0	$aSCOPE ;$v 29
	⩾0	$aAccess guides
	⩾0	$aEdmonton area series report ;$vno. 37

490   R   Series Untraced or Traced Differently. This field is used to record a series that is not traced in the way that it is found on the title page. If the series is to be traced, then the established version of the heading will be recorded in field 830.

Subfields	$a	R	Series statement
	$v	R	Volume or number
Indicators	1		Type of tracing
			0 - Series not traced
			1 - Series traced differently
	2		Blank
Example	1⩾		$aEarly English Text Society ;$vno. 285
	1⩾		$aMan and nature ;$v1981

0♭ $aPrentice-Hall contemporary topics in accounting
series

A series traced differently is placed in field 830. For the two examples given above the 830 entries are:

830 0♭ $aEarly English Text Society (Series).$pOriginal series ;$v
285.
830 0♭ $aMan and nature (Lincoln, Mass.) ;$v1981.

Notes (500 Level)

There are a large of number of 5XX fields to accommodate notes in both the serials and monographs formats of MARC. The most commonly used fields are described below.

500 R General Note. This field should be used for all notes other than the ones designated for the other '500' level fields.

Subfields $a   R   General note

Indicators   Blank

Example $a"Based on material presented at a national conference, Accounting for Inflation--Challenge for Business, conducted by Touche Ross & Co. and Financial Post Conferences in December 1974."-- 4th prelim. page.

$aIncludes index.

$aWith teacher's guide.

504 R Bibliography Note. This field contains notes which indicate the work has a bibliography. Notes about discographies and filmographies should also be included in this field.

Subfields $a   Bibliography/discography note

Indicators   Blank

Example $aIncludes bibliographies and index.
$aIncludes bibliographical references and index.
$aBibliography: p. 416-417.

505 Contents Note. This field is used primarily to describe the contents of multi-volume works. On cards being converted in a recon project the information may be preceded by the word "Contents:"; this should be omitted when coding the MARC record.

Subfields	$a	Contents note
Indicators	1	0 - Contents (complete)
		1 - Contents (incomplete)
		2 - Partial contents
	2	Blank
Example	2ƀ	$av. 1 -- v.2. The acquisitors.
	1ƀ	$av. 1. Report -- v. 3. Overseas systems of compensation.
	0ƀ	$apt. 1. The cause of liberty (24 min.) -- pt. 2. The impossible war (25 min.)

In a full MARC record there are many other note fields, but the ones described above are the most common and can be used to accommodate the information that a small- or medium-sized library requires. If a specific note field does not seem appropriate, then use the General Note field, 500. One other note field is provided for local notes and information that is specific to the library holding that particular title.

590 R Local Note.

Subfields	$a	Local note
Indicators	Blank	
Example	$aLibrary copy signed by author.	

Subject Entries (600 Level)

In a recon project, all subject entries will be found near the bottom of the card in the tracings area and are identified by an Arabic number. Only the text, and not the consecutive Arabic numbers, should be coded and entered into the MARC record. The recon operator or cataloger must identify which type of subject heading is being used in order to code the fields correctly. The choices are described below.

Subfields $x, $y, and $z in the 600 level fields are generally used to indicate "dashed" subdivisions of subject headings.

600 R Subject Heading—Personal Name. This field is used for any subject heading which is a personal name. The form of the name will be the same as if the person was the main entry in field 100, or an added personal entry in field 700. Typically this field is used for the subjects of biographies, autobiographies, and literary criticism.

Subfields	$a		Name (surname and forenames)
	$q		Expansion of initials in parenthesis
	$b		Number
	$c	R	Titles or other words associated with name
	$d		Date
	$t		Title of work
	$k		Form subheading
	$x	R	General subdivision
	$y	R	Period subdivision (chronological)
	$z	R	Geographic subdivision

Indicators	1		Type of personal name
		0	- Forename
		<u>1</u>	<u>- Single surname</u>
		2	- Multiple surname
		3	- Name of the family
	2		Source of subject heading
		<u>0</u>	<u>- LC subject heading</u>
		4	- Other subject heading
		5	- NLC - English subject heading
		6	- NLC - French subject heading

Examples	10	$aJenkins, Peter,$d1951-$xJourneys$zChina.
	10	$aFerraro, Geraldine.
	10	$aDavidson, Donald,$d1917-$tEssays on actions and events.
	14	$aDavidson, Donald,$d1917-$xCriticism and interpretation.
	14	$aNicholas$bII,$cEmperor of Russia,$d1868-1918.
	10	$aShakespeare, William,$d1564-1616.

610 R Subject Heading—Corporate Name. This field is used for any subject heading that represents the name of a corporate body, government agency, or other organization. The coding for this field is similar to the coding for the fields for Main entry - Corporate name (110) and Added entry - Corporate name (710).

Subfields	$a		Name
	$b	R	Subheading
	$d	R	Date (of conference, meeting or treaty)
	$c		Place (of conference, or meeting)
	$t		Title of work
	$k	R	Form subheading
	$x	R	General subdivision
	$y	R	Period subdivision (chronological)
	$z	R	Place subdivision

Indicators	1	Type of coporate name

	0	- Surname (inverted)
	1	- Place or place and name
	2	- Name (direct order)

	2	Source of subject heading

	0	- LC subject heading
	4	- Other subject heading
	5	- NLC - English subject heading
	6	- NLC - French subject heading

Examples	10	$aUnited States.$bCongress.$bHouse. $xHistory.
	10	$aSoviet Union.$kTreaties, etc.$bUnited States,$d1972 May 26 (ABM).
	10	$aUnited States.$bArmy$xHistory$yCivil War, 1861-1865.
	20	$aCanadian Open Golf Championship Tournament $d(1968 :$cToronto, Ont.)

611 R Subject Heading - Conference or Meeting. If a conference is the subject of a book, as opposed to the main entry, then the established name of the conference should be coded for the 611 field.

Subfields	$a	Name
	$q	Name if entry element under place
	$d	Date (of conference or meeting)
	$c	Place (of conference, or meeting)
	$n	Number or designation
	$t	Title of work

$k		Form subheading
$x	R	General subdivision
$y	R	Period subdivision (chronological)
$z	R	Place subdivision

| Indicators | 1 | Type of Conference or meeting name |
| | | |

0 - Surname (inverted)
1 - Place or place and name
2 - Name (direct order)

2 Source of subject heading

0 - LC subject heading
4 - Other subject heading
5 - NLC - English subject heading
6 - NLC - French subject heading

| Examples | 20 | $aConference on Techical Information Center Administration$n(3rd :$d1966 :$cPhiladelphia, Pa.) |
| | 20 | $aSymposium of Glaucoma$d(1966 :$cNew Orleans, La.) |

630 R Subject Heading—Uniform Title Heading. If a work, such as the Bible, is the subject of the book being cataloged, then this field would be used for the subject headings to describe the contents.

Subfields	$a		Uniform title heading
	$t		Title of work
	$k		Form subheading
	$l		Language
	$p	R	Name of part/section (of the work)
	$x	R	General subdivision
	$y	R	Period subdivision (chronological)
	$z	R	Place subdivision

| Indicators | 1 | Non-filing characters |

0-9 - Number of characters ignored in filing

2 Source of subject heading

0 - LC subject heading
4 - Other subject heading
5 - NLC - English subject heading
6 - NLC - French subject heading

Examples	00	$aBible.$lEnglish$xVersions$xNew English.
	00	$aDead Sea scrolls.
	45	$aThe Studio magazine.$pContemporary paintings$xPeriodicals.

This field is often used when describing books about motion pictures, or radio and television programs. It is generally used for works where the subject of the book would be a uniform title main entry or use the 240 uniform title field.

650 R Subject Heading—Topical.

Subfields	$a		Topical subject heading
	$x	R	General subdivision
	$y	R	Period subdivision (chronological)
	$z	R	Place subdivision

Indicators	1	Blank
	2	Source of subject heading

	0	- LC subject heading
	4	- Other subject heading
	5	- NLC - English subject heading
	6	- NLC - French subject heading

Examples	ʰ0	$aEducational accountability.
	ʰ0	$aTax planning$zUnited States.
	ʰ0	$aAccounting$xData processing.
	ʰ0	$aChurch and state in Germany$y20th century.
	ʰ0	$aHorses$xJuvenile fiction.
	ʰ6	$aProfesseurs (Enseignement superieur) $zQuebec (Province)$zMontreal$xCas, Etudes de.
	ʰ0	$aPostage stamps$zCanada.
	ʰ6	$aTimbres-poste$zCanada.
	ʰ5	$aInuit$zCanada$xLegal status, laws, etc.$xHistory.

651 R Subject Heading—Geographic. This field is used for subject headings that refer to places, natural features, regions, sites, parks, and political jurisdictions. The exception to using this heading is for political jurisdictions that are subdivided by names or organizations as these are considered to be corporate names and field 610 should be used. For example, "United States--Politics and government" is a geographic subject heading but "United States. Congress. House—History" is a corporate name subject heading. Another consideration for subject headings with geographic applications are those with geographic subdivisions which would be placed in 650, topical subject headings. An example of this type of heading would be "Legislators--United States—Biography."

Subfields	$a		Geographic name
	$x	R	General subdivision
	$y	R	Period subdivision (chronological)
	$z	R	Place subdivision

Indicators	1	Blank	
	2	0	- LC subject heading
		4	- Other subject heading
		5	- NLC - English subject heading
		6	- NLC - French subject heading

Examples	ƀ0	$aGermany$xPolitics and government$y1918-1933.
	ƀ0	$aFrance$xHistory$ySecond Republic, 1848-1852$xArt.
	ƀ0	$aLondon (England)$xDescription$y1981- $xGuide-books.
	ƀ5	$aCanada$xSocial conditions$y1971-

Added Entries (700 Level)

If MARC records are being created as part of a recon project from the shelf-list cards, all these entries will be found in the tracings area of the card and identified by a Roman numeral. The Roman numeral should not be included in the MARC record. Much of the coding for these fields corresponds to the equivalent field in the main entries; however there is an important difference. Each of the 7XX fields can be repeated as many times as necessary, while traditionally there can only be one 1XX field.

Most automated library systems create indexes from the combined 1XX and 7XX fields without distinguishing between the main and added entries. Correct labelling of the fields is important so that personal authors can be distinguished from corporate ones, since searches by these different types of authors will often be represented by different menu choices in the online catalog. If MARC records are used to create cards, for example with one of the CD-ROM products, the 7XX fields will be printed above the unit card for filing purposes.

The use of the second indicator is the same for all the fields in the 7XX group:

Indicators	1		Varies for each field and corresponds to its use in the 1XX fields for the author added entries
	2	0	- alternative entry indicates an entry such as a joint author, corporate sponsors, etc. In the card catalog these entries could have been subfiled by title.

| 2 (cont.) | 1 | - secondary entry is generally used for works that would have been subfiled by main entry in a card catalog. For example author/title added entries, and added entries for lesser persons (e.g., editors, illustrators) in the work where the main entry is a personal name. |
| | 2 | - analytical entry, is used for a sub-unit of work contained in the main work. |

700 R Added Entry - Personal Name. In this field enter any additional personal names associated with the creation of the work. The subfield coding for this field is the same as for the Main entry - Personal name (100). An author/title added entry is accommodated by using the subfield code '$t' in front of the title.

Subfields	$a		Name
	$q		Expansion of initials in parenthesis
	$b		Number
	$c	R	Titles or other words associated with name
	$d		Date
	$e		Relator (e.g., editor, illustrator etc.)
	$t		Title of work

Indicators	1	Type of personal name
	0	- Forename
	1	- Single surname
	2	- Multiple surname
	3	- Name of the family
	2	Type of entry
	0	- Alternative entry
	1	- Secondary entry
	2	- Analytical entry

Example	11	$aKaluza, Henry J.,$d1930-$tAccounting : a systems approach.
	10	$aHoward, Murray B.
	10	$aHopkins, Claude C.,$d1866-1932.
	10	$aLindheim, Barbara L.$ejoint author.
	11	$aSpurrier, Steven.$tFrench country wines.
	11	$aMillar, Kenneth,$d1915-$tMoving target.

710 R Added Entry—Corporate Name. In this field any additional corporate names associated with the creation of the work are entered. The subfield coding for this field is the same as for the Main Entry - Corporate Name (110). An author/title added entry is accommodated by using the subfield label '$t' in front of the title.

Subfields	$a		Name
	$b	R	Subheading
	$d	R	Date
	$c		Place
	$e		Relator
	$t		Title of work

Indicators	1	Type of corporate name
		0 — Surname (inverted)
		1 — Place or place and name
		2 — Name (direct order)
	2	Type of entry
		0 — Alternative entry
		1 — Secondary entry
		2 — Analytical entry

Example	20	$aChartered Society of Physiotherapy (Great Britain)
	20	$aCongressional Medal of Honor Society of the United States of America.
	20	$aLaw Society of Upper Canada.
	21	$aFoundation for Inner Peace.$tA course in miracles.
	21	$aBritish Broadcasting Corporation. $bContinuing Education Advisory Council.
	11	$aUnited States.$bArmy Map Service.

711 R Added Entry—Conference or Meeting. Enter here any tracing or added entry which is the name of a conference, meeting, or symposium. In addition to examples below, the ones in field 111, Main entry - Conference or Meeting, should be consulted.

Subfields	$a		Name
	$q		Name if entry element ($a) under place
	$d		Date
	$c		Place
	$n	R	Number of part / section / conference
	$t		Title of work

Indicators	1	Type of conference or meeting

0	- Surname (inverted)
1	- Place or place and name
<u>2</u>	<u>- Name (direct order)</u>

	2	Type of entry

<u>0</u>	<u>- Alternative entry</u>
1	- Secondary entry
2	- Analytical entry

Example	20	$aSymposium on the Life and Thought of Abraham Joshua Heschel$d(1983 :$cSaint Joseph, Minn.)
	21	$aVatican Council$n(2nd :$d1962-1965)
	20	$aCanadian Open Golf Championship Tournament$d(1958 :$cToronto)

730 R Added Entry—Uniform Title Heading. This field is used to record a uniform title heading associated with the work but not used as the main entry.

Subfields	$a		Uniform title heading
	$t		Title of the work
	$p	R	Name of part / section (of a work)

Indicators	1	Non-filing characters
		0-9 - Number of characters ignored in filing
	2	Type of entry

<u>0</u>	<u>- Alternative entry</u>
1	- Secondary entry
2	- Analytical entry

Example	01	$aBalliol College record.$pSupplement.
	02	$aBible.$pO.T.$pJudges V.

740 Added Entry—Title Traced Differently. This field is used for alternative title tracings and should not be confused with a title added entry, which is identified by the first indicator in field 245 being set to '1'. Title added entries on printed cards are preceded by a Roman numeral and the word "Title:".

Subfields	$a	Title traced differently

Indicators	1	Non-filing characters

0-9   - Number of characters ignored in filing

         2   Type of entry

              <u>0</u>   <u>- Alternative entry</u>
              1   - Secondary entry
              2   - Analytical entry

Note the reversal of indicator use for the number of characters ignored in filing. In field 245 the second indicator is used for this purpose.

Examples	01	$aAV troubleshooter.
	01	$aWine cellar book.
	01	$aA-ten Thunderbolt 2.
	01	$aA-10 Thunderbolt two.

In the first example the 245 $a subfield contained the title *A/V troubleshooter,* which would file quite differently from 'AV' under computer filing rules, so the cataloger provides a secondary access point through the 740 field. In the second example, the 245 $a subfield contained the title *The Academie du vin wine cellar book,* but it is likely that most people would know the book as *The wine cellar book,* hence the added entry. The remaining examples are good examples of additional entries that are needed because computer filing is literal, and will not take into account the intellectual interpretations and rules that have always been used to file and search in a manual card catalog.

Other examples of when a 740 title added entry is appropriate include:

              245 04 $aThe listing attic ; The unstrung harp /$cby Edward Gorey
              740 01 $aListing attic.
              740 01 $aUnstrung harp.
and,

              503 ƀƀ $aFormerly: Five nation study
              740 01 $aFive nation study

Series Added Entries (800 Level)

The 8XX fields are used for the correct form of tracing for traced series described in the 490 field. Where appropriate, the examples here show the 490 "version" of the tracing or a related main entry from the 1XX level.

830 R Series Added Entry—Title and Uniform Title. Since the implementation of *AACR2*, this field has been used for both title and uniform title series added entry. The field 840 is no longer used for title series entries.

Subfields $a   Uniform title
                $n   R   Number or designation
                $p   R   Part or section
                $v   Volume or number

Indicators   1   Blank
                2   Non-filing characters

                0-9   - Number of characters ignored in filing

Examples   ₩0 $aEarly English Text Society (Series).$pOriginal series ;$v
                         285.
                ₩0 $aMan and nature (Lincoln, Mass.) ;$v1981.

850 R Holdings [serials format]. When cataloging serials, the information about the library's actual holdings of a title, as compared with the publication dates and volumes in field 362, is entered in this field. This is where a summary statement about "items held" is recorded and it has a different meaning from "items published," which are recorded in field 362.

Subfields $a   Reporting library
                $b   Holdings (summary only)
                $d   Inclusive dates
                $e   Retention statement

Indicators   Blank

Example $aCaOONL$b1-12, 14- ;$d1951-62, 1964-

Reviewing this summary of the essential MARC fields, it is possible to see that there is a logical pattern to the way that tag numbers are assigned. That is, where appropriate, the first number of the tag represents the group or level of the variable length fields, and then for 1XX, 4XX, 6XX, 7XX, and 8XX fields, the second and third digits are assigned as follows:

X00   represents a personal name
X10   represents a coporate name
X11   represents a conference of meeting
X30 or X40   represents a title and/or uniform title entry

Local Holdings Fields

The portion of the record that is unique to the library using the record is called the local holdings field. This is the field where the library records the actual call number on its copies of the title, the number of copies and volumes owned by the library, and their locations. The number used to tag the local holdings fields varies from system to system, and some examples are given here. The most important thing in recording this information is to establish a pattern for the subfields and then to use it consistently. All equivalent pieces of information in this, or any other field, must have consistent field and subfield labelling from record to record; otherwise the processing programs will not create consistent displays and retrieval keys. If the use of fields and subfields is consistent, then the programs that are used to load MARC records into local library systems can usually be customized to handle variations in usage.

The purpose of the local holdings fields is to record the exact location and physical volume holdings for the library, and to store this information in a format that can be used to generate item level information for display in online catalogs and for circulation systems. One might think of the local holdings field as replacing all the pencilled notes that we used to put on the back of the shelf-list card.

Opinions differ about whether or not to include barcode numbers in local holdings fields. In general the bibliographic utilities discourage users from including barcode numbers in their records when they are stored in the utility databases. Barcode information is more appropriately created and stored when the library is loading records into a local system or doing an in-house recon project. If you do wish to include barcode information at the time of cataloging or recon, then there are subfields in the local holding field to accommodate it.

The following examples are provided for guidance. Each library should establish correct use of the local holdings field with their system vendor. If a system has not been selected but recon is commencing, then use one of the examples given here.

Both OCLC and Utlas provide complex coding instructions for use of local holdings fields. Much of the complexity is because of the need to use this information in creating cards, labels, and other products. Simplified versions are described here and should be adequate for creating records for local online systems.

Following are some simple examples from automated library systems. These are provided to show the type of information that is kept in the local holdings field. It is essential that you check with the appropriate system vendor before starting to create a local holdings field.

OCLC: 049, 090 and 092

049 Local holdings

Subfields	$a	Holding library code
	$c	Copy statement

090 Locally assigned LC-type call number

Subfields	$a	LC class number
	$b	Cutter number or book number

092 Locally assigned Dewey call number

Subfields	$a	Dewey Decimal Classification Number
	$b	Book number

Utlas: 090

Indicators	Blank

Subfields	$a	call number
	$b	location
	$f	collection
	$s	shelving location within collection
	$c	copy
	$g	non-date volume designation
	$h	date volume designation

Bibliofile for use with multiLIS: 090

Subfields	$a	call number
	$b	location
	$c	copy
	$d	volume
	$v	barcode number

Library Services Centre, Ontario: 966

Subfields	$l	Branch code
	$c	Copy
	$b	Bar code
	$d	Volume
	$s	Call number
	$w	Source of purchase
	$p	Price
	$x	Date
	$m	Binding
	$n	Copy note

As you can see, there is little consistency in the use of local holdings fields. However, this is an essential field, as it is where you customize a cataloging record to reflect the library's holdings. For this reason you should establish a consistent use for the field in your library, document it, and ensure that it is used correctly.

Conclusion

In order to bring the information in this chapter together, some records from the Library of Congress files are shown below. These records were obtained from the BiblioFile version of Library of Congress MARC database so the field names are transcribed as found on that system. As you can see, the field descriptions, similar to those you will find in many MARC-based systems, make the information more comprehensible to the uninitiated. In this example we have used '$' as the subfield delimiter. In a BiblioFile record you will see '▼' as the delimiter.

Record Hdr	000		nam8a
Control #	001		87045087
	008		870326s1987░░░░nyu░░░░░░░░░░░░░░░0░eng░d
ISBN	020		$a006015785 :$c$17.95
Cat. Source	040		$aDNLM/DLC$cDLC
LC Call	050	0░	$aRC86.7.G63$bZ54 1987
NLM Call	060		$aWZ 100 G6184
Dewey Class	082	0░	$a616/.025/0924$219
Local call #090	00		$a616.025$bNF$v31962000000582
ME:Pers Name	100	10	$aZiegler, Edward.
Title	245	10	$aEmergency doctor / $cby Edward Ziegler in cooperation with Lewis R. Goldfrank.
Edition	250		$a1st ed.
Imprint	260	0░	$aNew York :$bHarper & Row,$cc1987.
Phys Descrpt	300		$ap. cm.
Subj:Pers	600	10	$aGoldfrank, Lewis R.,$d1941-
Subj:Topical	650	░0	$aEmergency physicians$zNewYork $xBiography.
Subj:Topical	650	░0	$aEmergency medicine$xCase studies.
Subj:Corp	610	20	$aBellevue Hospital
AE:Pers Name	700	10	$aGoldfrank, Lewis R.,$d1941-

Some comments are in order:

008 indicates that this is a single-volume work, published in 1987 in New York. It is a nonfiction work in English, with a cataloging source other than Library of Congress.

040 indicates that the National Library of Medicine cataloged this work prior to Library of Congress adopting the record.

060 is the National Library of Medicine call number, which will generally be ignored by small libraries unless that happens to be the classification scheme used.

082 was used as the classification number for the library's own copy of the work, but it was trancated at the '/' [slash] mark for the library's use.

Information about the library's holdings, including the local call number, has been added in field 090. This library has decided to include the barcode number in the $v subfield, according to rules provided by the local system vendor. Some vendors provide the facility to indicate breaks in the call number for label or card printing by inserting ';' [colons], or '/' [slash]. Check your system manual for details on this feature.

The projected publication date of this work is September 1987 (indicating this is a Cataloging in Publication record), and therefore physical description field is not yet completed. The library deriving this record would complete field 300 from the work in hand.

The rest of the record requires little explanation except to point out that within each group or level of fields they can be entered in any order. In the subject heading fields, 600 level, the headings are not in numerical order, but this is quite acceptable.

The remaining two examples are variations on the same theme, and are provided to show some of the other options in coding bibliographic information for online cataloging.

Record Hdr	000		nam8a
Control #	001		87003475
	008		870513s1987⍰⍰⍰mnu⍰⍰⍰j⍰⍰⍰⍰⍰⍰⍰0⍰eng⍰d
ISBN	020		$a0822516764 (lib. bdg.) :c8.95
LC Call	050	0⍰	$aDS796.H75$bM34 1987
Dewey Class	082	0⍰	$a951/.25$219
Local call #	090	00	$a951.25$bANF
ME:Pers Name	100	10	$aMcKenna, Nancy Durrell
Title	245	12	$aA family in Hong Kong /$bNancy Durrell McKenna.
Imprint	260	0⍰	$aMinneapolis :$bLerner Publications co.,$c1987.
Projected Pub	263		$a8709
Phys Descrpt	300		$ap. cm.
Series:Title	440	0	$aFamilies the world over
Abstract	520		$aDescribes the life of ten-year-old Tse Yik Ming who lives in an apartment building in Hong Kong.
Subj:Geog	651	⍰0	$aHong Kong$xSocial life and customs $xJuvenile literature
Subj:Topical	650	⍰0	$aFamily$zHong Kong$xJuvenile literature.
Subj:Topical	650	⍰1	$aFamily life$zHong Kong.
Subj:Geog	651	⍰1	$aHong Kong$xSocial life and customs.

Record Hdr	000		nam8a
Control #	001		87401133
	008		870504s1980ⱶⱶⱶcouⱶⱶⱶⱶⱶⱶⱶⱶⱶⱶⱶⱶ0ⱶengⱶ
LC Call	050	0ⱶ	$aCS71.E468$b1980
Dewey Class	082	0ⱶ	$a929/.2/0973$219
Local call #	090	00	$aCS71.E468 1980$ANF
ME:Pers Name	100	10	$aElliott, Elsie,$d1914-
Title	245	10	$aTimes to remember /$ccompiled and written in part by Elsie Elliott.
Imprint	260	0ⱶ	$aDenver, Colo. :$bE. Elliott,$cc1980.
Phys Descrpt	300		$ap. cm.
Note:General	500		$a"Up-date, corrections, and additions to Times to Remember, 24 March 1987" (3 leaves) inserted.
Subj:Pers	600	30	$aElliott family.
Subj:Pers	600	30	$aGardner family.
Subj:Pers	600	30	$aCraig family.

Checklist:
MARC Bibliographic Records

The MARC bibliographic record consists of:

Leader   Information provided to the application program about how to process the record

Directory   Detailed information about the layout of the record

Variable length control fields

001   Control number

005   Date and Time of Latest Transaction

007   Physical description fixed field

008   Fixed length data elements—general information

Variable length fields

010   Library of Congress Card Number

016   National Library of Canada Bibliographic Control Number

020   International Standard Book Number

035   Local System Control Number

040   Cataloging Source

050   LC Call Number

082   Dewey Decimal Classification Number

Main entry headings

100   Personal Name

110   Corporate Name

111   Conference or Meeting

130   Uniform Title

Title / Imprint entries

240   Uniform Title

245   Title Statement

250   Edition Statement

260   Imprint / Release

263   Projected Publication Date

Physical description

300   Collation

310   Current Frequency [serials only]

362   Dates of Publication and Volume Designations [serials only]

Series entries

440   Series title (Traced)

490   Series Untraced or Traced Differently

Notes

500   General Note

504   Bibliography Note

505   Contents Note

590   Local Note

Subject entries

600   Personal Name

610   Corporate Name

611   Conference or Meeting

630   Uniform Title Heading

650   Topical Subject Heading

651   Geographic

Added entries

700   Personal Name

710   Corporate Name

711   Conference or Meeting

730   Uniform Title Heading

740   Title Traced Differently

Series added entries

830   Title and Uniform Title

850   Holdings [serials only]

Further Reading

Byrne, Deborah. "The Much-Misunderstood MARC Fixed Field." *Action for Libraries* 13 (February 1987): 4; 13 (March 1987): 4-5.

Library of Congress. Automated Systems Office. *MARC Formats for Bibliographic Data.* Washington, DC: Library of Congress, 1980- . Looseleaf.

Litchfield, Charles A., and Marilyn L. "Coded Holdings: A Primer for New Users." *Serials Review* 14, no. 1-2 (1988): 81-88.

National Library of Canada. *Canadian MARC Communication Format: Mini-MARC.* Ottawa: National Library of Canada, 1982.

———. *Canadian MARC Communication Format: Minimal Level.* Ottawa: National Library of Canada, 1987.

———. Canadian MARC Office. *Canadian MARC Communications Format: Bibliographic Data.* Ottawa: National Library of Canada, 1988- . Looseleaf. (DSS cat. no. SN214/1988E)

12
MARC Authority Records

The previous chapter discussed the use of MARC formats for bibliographic records. Some library systems also support the use of authority records which can be linked to bibliographic records in order to maintain consistency in the use of certain headings.

Authority records are important in online library systems, not only to maintain consistent headings for displays, but also to ensure that all records containing a particular author, series, or subject are retrieved by a single search statement. Bibliographic databases, like card catalogs, that do not incorporate authority control will sometimes show a variety of headings in response to a search. In the manual environment we were able to compensate for minor variations on cards by interfiling them. The computer is less forgiving and an online search that retrieves variations in a particular heading requires that the user check each of the associated hit lists to find the required title. Worse still, the search may fail to find all appropriate items because a mistake in a heading meant that the computer found no match at all.

For example a search for plays by the author William Shakespeare could be entered as "AU=Shakespeare W*". If the library does not control headings carefully, the following display may result:

Shakespeare, William, L564-1616.	[digit in name and letter in date]
Shakespeare, Wiliam, 1564-1614.	[mis-spelled name]
Shakespeare, William, 1546-1614.	
Shakespeare, William, 1554-1616.	[incorrect dates]
Shakespeare, William, 1554-1606.	
Shakespeare, William, 1564-1616.	[correct heading]

The final heading in the above list is the correct heading, all the others are actual, but incorrect, headings that were found by searching a university library system's online union catalog where some of the branch libraries do not use authority control. The same types of problems can occur with subject headings. For example, a search for books London, England, SU=London E*, yielded:

London (Eng.)
London (England)

With proper authority control, the searches should have yielded "Shakespeare, William, 1564-1616" and "London (England)" with no variations.

Authority control is used to maintain consistency of personal and corporate author headings, conference and meeting names, subject headings, series headings, and uniform titles. The diagram below illustrates the concept of authority control in the online environment. Authority control implies that the correct form of the heading only needs to be stored in the authority record, and all uses of that heading are maintained through links to the appropriate bibliographic record.

The diagram on the following page shows graphically the concept of storing a heading once and then linking it to bibliographic records using that heading.

In addition to maintaining consistency in the database, this method of only storing the heading once is much more efficient for making global changes to a heading. You no longer have to change every record in which the heading occurs. A change to the authority record will be reflected in every bibliographic record that is linked to the heading. Storing the heading only once is also a more efficient way of using disk storage space in the computer system.

The MARC authority record format also provides for the establishment of "see" and "see also" references. In the eleventh edition of *LCSH*, "see" and "see also" references have been replaced by the expressions commonly used in thesauri. Instead of "see" references the instruction "Use" refers the user to the established heading. "UF" or "Used for" refers to terms that are unused synonyms for the "Used" term. The example below uses the nomenclature of the eleventh edition. The fields that are used in each authority record for these references contain only headings that relate to the authorized heading.

In *LCSH* the following heading is established:

Eskimos

UF	Eskimauan Indians
	Esquimaux
	Innuit
	Inuit
BT	Arctic races
	Indians of North America
NT	Aleuts
	Chugach Eskimos

BIBLIOGRAPHIC RECORDS

AUTHORITY RECORD

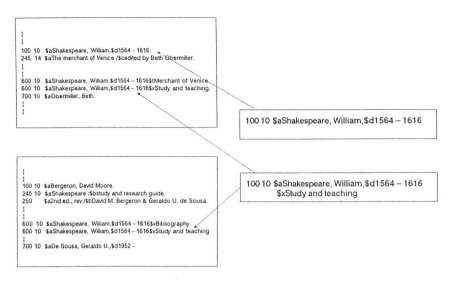

When the records are actually stored in the database, text in the fields that are under authority control will be replaced with pointers to where that same text is stored in the authority record.

> Igloos
> Kaniagmuit (Eskimo tribe)
> Kuuvanmiit Eskimos
> Ugalakmiut Indians
> Utkuhigjalingmiut (Eskimo people)

The equivalent heading in *Canadian Subject Headings* (*CSH*) 2nd. edition to *LCSH* use of Eskimos is:

Inuit—Canada

> See references from:
> Canada--Inuit
> Eskimos—Canada [*LCSH*]
> Eskimauan Indians—Canada
> Esquimaux—Canada
> Innuit—Canada
>
> See also:
> Canada—Native races
> Indians of North America—Canada

These two opposing headings have been chosen because they are good examples of how automated authority control can be used to maintain preferred headings in an individual library's database. A description of this process follows at the end of this chapter, after the field-by-field guide to authority records.

Until recently there was very little need to understand the structure of authority records unless you were using a bibliographic utility for database creation. However, in 1988 the Library of Congress released its first CD-ROM product, CDMARC Subjects. The introduction of this product and its planned companion—CDMARC Names—mean that more libraries will have access to MARC authority records and will want to incorporate them into their local online catalogs. In anticipation of the move to greater use of authorities by smaller libraries, we have decided to include a brief outline of MARC authority records and their uses.

We are going to review the fields and layout of a MARC authority record first. There are many similarities to the MARC bibliographic record structure that was described in the previous chapter. Following the layout established in the previous chapter, each field is described in terms of its use, subfields, and indicators, and examples are provided.

Components of the MARC Authority Record

Leader and Directory

The leader and directory are constructed in the same way as for a bibliographic record. Position 6 of the leader has the value 'z,' which indicates that the record is an authority record.

Position 17 of the leader of an authority record represents the encoding level of the record:

n - complete authority record
o - incomplete authority record

Variable Length Control Fields

001 Control Number. As in the bibliographic format, this field contains the control number assigned by the organization creating, using, or distributing the record.

Examples   nrb8600000001b
                            shb850082771b

This field is be generated by the automated system.

005 Date and Time of Latest Transaction. The date and time provide important information for processing the record and are used to verify updates and changes to the catalog. These elements are assigned by the automated library system and changed each time the record is modified and refiled.

008 Fixed-length Data Elements. Similar in structure to the 008 field in the bibliographic record, this field has no subfield codes or indicators. The elements of the field are defined by their position in the field. There are forty character positions (00-39) that provide coded information about the record as a whole or about special aspects of the 1XX headings or 4XX/5XX tracing fields. These coded data elements are potentially useful for online retrieval and general catalog management purposes. When deriving an authority record, this field should be accepted without changes.

Variable Length Fields (010-899)

010 Library of Congress Authority Control Number. This is an eight-digit number, preceded by three blanks or an alphabetic prefix, and followed by a variable number of characters as required.

Subfields	$a	LC authority control number
Indicators	Blank	
Examples	$a	nbb84002822
	$a	anb50039908

In the first example the original control number would have been n84-2822, similarly an5-39908 is entered as 50039908.

040 Record Source. This field is used to indicate the source of the authority record, typically Library of Congress, National Library of Canada, etc., and it also indicates any other agency that may have modified the original authority record.

Subfields	$a		Original cataloging agency code
	$d	R	Modifying agency
Indicators	Blank		
Example	$aDLC		
	$aDNLM		
	$aCaOONL		
	$aCaOONL$dCaOTU		
	$aBNB		

These symbols represent Library of Congress, National Library of Medicine, National Library of Canada, University of Toronto, and British National Bibliography respectively. In the fourth example, the University of Toronto had modified an authority record that was supplied by the National Library of Canada. The user should maintain a record of codes and the hierarchy for accepting authority records.

Established Headings (100 Level)

The entries in the 100 level fields, 1XX, of an authority record represent the established, or authorized, versions of headings that can be used in bibliographic records.

100   Established Heading—Personal Name. Used for personal names as established headings. Headings in this field will be used to control personal names in the following fields in the bibliographic record:

100	Main Entry - Personal Name
600	Subject Entry - Personal Name
700	Added Entry - Personal Name

Subfields	$a		Name (surnames and forenames)
	$q		Expansion of initials in parenthesis, i.e., a qualification of the name in fuller form
	$b		Number (roman numerals)
	$c	R	Titles or other words associated with name
	$d		Date
Indicators	1		Type of personal name entry element

	0	- Forename
	1	- Single surname
	2	- Multiple surname
	3	- Name of the family

	2	Non-filing characters

	0-9	- Number of non-filing characters present

Examples	10	$aShakespeare, William,$d1564-1616.
	10	$aRichey, Robert W.$q(Robert William)$d1912-
	10	$aDickens, Charles.
	20	$aVaughan Williams, Ralph,$d1872-1958.
	30	$aNormandy, Dukes of.

110 Established Heading—Corporate name. Enter in this field any established or authorized corporate name. Entries in this field will be used to control entries in the following bibliographic fields:

110   Main Entry - Corporate name
610   Subject Entry - Corporate Name
710   Added Entry - Corporate Name

Subfields	$a		Name
	$b	R	Subheading (each subordinate unit in the hierarchy of the organization)
	$d	R	Date
	$c		Place
	$k		Form subheading

Indicators	1	Type of corporate name entry element

	0	- Surname (inverted)
	1	- Place or place and name
	2	- Name (direct order)

	2	Non-filing characters

	0-9	- Number of non-filing characters present

Examples	20	$aWinrock International Institute for International Development
	20	$aEmpire State Building (New York, N.Y.)
	10	$aBritish Columbia.$bFish and Wildlife Branch
	20	$aCatholic Church.$bConcilium Plenarium Americae Latinae$d(1899 :$cRome, Italy)

111 Established Heading—Conference or Meeting. This field is used for the established name of a conference or meeting. Under authority control it will be used to control the following fields in the bibliographic record:

111   Main Entry - Conference or Meeting
611   Subject Entry - Conference or Meeting
711   Added Entry - Conference or Meeting

Subfields	$a	Name of meeting or place element
	$q	Name if entry element ($a) under place
	$d	Date
	$c	Place
	$n	Number of part/section/meeting

Indicators	1	Type of meeting name entry element

		0	- Surname (inverted)
		1	- Place or place and name
		2	- Name (direct order)

	2	Non-filing characters

		0-9	- Number of non-filing characters present

Examples	20	$aCentral Australian Gold Exploration Company Expedition$d(1930)
	20	$aSymposium on Finite Element Methods in Geotechnical Engineering$d(1972 :$cVicksburg, Miss.)

130 Established Heading—Uniform Title. This field is used for the established version of all uniform titles. In the bibliographic record, the following fields will be controlled by this authority record field:

130	Main Entry - Uniform Title
630	Subject Entry - Uniform Title
730	Added Entry - Uniform Title
830	Series Added Entry - Title and Uniform Title

Subfields	$a		Uniform title heading
	$p	R	Part or section
	$t		Title of the work
	$k	R	Form subheading

Indicators	1	Blank

	2	Non-filing characters

		0-9	- Number of non-filing characters present

Examples	ƀ0	$aBible.$pN.T.$pCorinthians, 1st.
	ƀ0	$aTen commandments

150 Established Heading—Topical Term. Entries in this field of the authority record will be used to control just one of the bibliographic fields: 650—Subject entry Topical Subject Heading.

Subfields	$a		Topical subject heading
	$x	R	General subdivision
	$y	R	Period subdivision (chronological)
	$z	R	Place subdivision

Indicators	1		Blank
	2		Non-filing characters

0-9   - Number of non-filing characters present

Examples	ƀ0	$aMen actors
	ƀ0	$aArchitecture, Modern$y19th century
	ƀ0	$aWater resources development$zKenya
	ƀ0	$aEskimos
	ƀ0	$aInuit$zCanada

We will be following the Eskimos/Inuit example throughout this section of the chapter. Depending on whether you use *LCSH* or *CSH*, either heading can be established as the preferred heading. However, having chosen which heading is to be used in your library, the appropriate references must be established in order to lead the user to the preferred heading.

151 Established Heading—Geographic Name. Like the 150 heading described above, this heading matches to one bibliographic field: 651 - Subject Entry - Geographic.

Subfields	$a		Geographic name
	$x	R	General subdivision
	$y	R	Period subdivision (chronological)
	$z	R	Place subdivision

Indicators	1		Blank
	2		Non-filing characters

0-9   - Number of non-filing characters present

Examples	ƀ0	$aCooper's Creek (Qld. and S.Aust.)
	ƀ0	$aAmazon River
	ƀ0	$aUnited States$xCensus, 2nd, 1800
	ƀ0	$aUnited States$xHistory$yCivil War, 1861-1865$xConscientious objectors
	ƀ0	$aUnited States$xBoundaries$zCanada
	ƀ0	$aDeveloping countries

The fields in the next two sections of the authority record, the see from and see also from headings, have the same basic layout as the corresponding field in the 1XX fields. For example, the personal name established heading, see from tracing and see also from tracing, all have the same subfield and indicator structure. The structure is repeated for each tracing described here in order to save the reader having to refer backwards and forwards in text while using this handbook. However, it is important to note that the layout of the record is logical, and consistent with the use of headings for various purposes. As noted before, the subfield structure is also consistent with corresponding fields in the MARC bibliographic record.

See from Tracings

The entries in the 4XX fields are for headings that are used as a see reference from an unestablished heading to the heading in the 1XX field of the authority record. These will be variant names and forms of a heading by which a person, organization, meeting, series, or subject might be known. The 4XX field is also sometimes used for different forms of names which may be found in older cataloging records. When the cataloger wishes to bring all items together under the latest version of the name or to ensure that incorrect headings are changed to the currently used forms, creating a 4XX reference makes it possible to correct headings in the bibliographic records. (This concept is shown graphically later in this chapter.) The alternative would be to enter publications under the name established at the time of publication and then to establish see also references using the 5XX fields that are described below. Some of the examples below are the variant forms of headings which were used as examples in 1XX fields described previously. The examples, at the end of this chapter, show complete authority records and the relationships between the various examples used in this field-by-field description.

All the 4XX fields are repeatable so that the cataloger can create as many references to the established heading as may be required.

400 R See From Tracing—Personal Name. This field contains a tracing for a personal name "see from reference." It is used to create a see reference from a personal name that is not used to an established heading.

Subfields	$a		Name (surnames and forenames)
	$q		Expansion of initials in parenthesis, i.e., a qualification of the name in fuller form
	$b		Number (roman numerals)
	$c	R	Titles or other words associated with name
	$d		Date

Indicators	1		Type of personal name

		0	- Forename
		1	- Single surname
		2	- Multiple surname
		3	- Name of the family

	2		Non-filing characters

		0-9	- Number of non-filing characters present

Examples	400	10	$aShakespeare, W.
	400	10	$aRichey, Robert William,$d1912-
	100	30	$aAnjou, House of
	400	30	$aAngio, House of

410 R See From Tracing—Corporate Name. This field contains a tracing for a corporate name "see from reference." It is used to create a see reference from an unused corporate name to an established heading.

Subfields	$a		Name
	$b	R	Subheading (each subordinate unit in the hierarchy of the organization)
	$d	R	Date
	$c		Place
	$k		Form subheading

Indicators	1		Type of corporate name

		0	- Surname (inverted)
		1	- Place or place and name
		2	- Name (direct order)

	2		Non-filing characters

		0-9	- Number of non-filing characters present

Examples	151	₿0	$aChinatown (San Francisco, Calif.)
	410	10	$aSan Francisco (Calif.).$bChinatown
	110	20	$aEastman Kodak Company
	410	20	$aKodak Company

411 R See From Tracing—Meeting Name. This field contains a tracing for a meeting or conference name "see from reference." It is used to create a see reference from an unused meeting name to an established heading in field 111 of the authority record.

Subfields	$a	Name of meeting or place element
	$q	Name if entry element ($a) under place
	$d	Date
	$c	Place
	$n	Number or designation

Indicators	1	Type of conference or meeting
		0 - Surname (inverted)
		1 - Place or place and name
		2 - Name (direct order)
	2	Non-filing characters
		0-9 - Number of non-filing characters present

Examples	111	20	$aCentral Australian Gold Exploration Company Expedition$d(1930)
	411	20	$aLasseter Expedition of 1930$d(1930)
	411	20	$aCentral Australian Gold Exploration Expedition

430 R See From Tracing—Uniform Title Heading. This field contains a tracing for a uniform title "see from reference." It is used to create a see reference from an unused uniform title to an established heading in field 130 of the authority record.

Subfields	$a	Uniform title heading
	$p	Part or section
	$t	Title of the work
	$k	Form subheading

Indicators	1	Blank
	2	Non-filing characters
		0-9 - Number of characters ignored in filing

Examples	130	ƀ0	$aBible.$pN.T.$pMatthew
	430	ƀ0	$aBible.$pN.T.$pMatthew VI, 9-13

450 R See From Tracing—Topical Term. This field contains a tracing for a topical subject heading term "see from reference." It is used to create a see reference from an unused topical term to an established heading in field 150 of the authority record.

Subfields	$a		Topical subject heading
	$x	R	General subdivision
	$y	R	Period subdivision (chronological)
	$z	R	Place subdivision

Indicators	1		Blank
	2		0-9 Non-filing characters

Examples	150	₿0	$aMen actors
	450	₿0	$aActors, Male
	450	₿0	$aMale actors
	150	₿0	$aAfrican drama (English)
	450	₿0	$aEnglish drama$xAfrican authors

This is where you would establish the "see from" references for the heading selected for Eskimos/Inuit. For example in a U.S. library using *LCSH*:

	450	₿0	$aEskmauan Indians
	450	₿0	$aInuit
	450	₿0	$aInnuit

will establish references from these terms to the correct term "Eskimos" so that if a user tried to do a subject search for the term "Inuit" s/he would be referred to the correct term automatically.

In a Canadian library, choosing to use "Inuit--Canada" as the subject heading for Eskimo people, the "see from" references would be different:

	450	₿0	$aEskimos$zCanada
	451	₿0	$aCanada$xInuit
	450	₿0	$aInnuit$zCanada

Searching "Eskimos" in a database established with "Inuit--Canada" as the heading will automatically refer the user to the preferred term in this library.

451 R See From Tracing—Geographic Name. This field contains a tracing for a see reference from a geographic name. It is used to create a see reference from a geographic name that is not used to an established heading in field 151 of the authority record.

Subfields	$a		Geographic name
	$x	R	General subdivision
	$y	R	Period subdivision (chronological)
	$z	R	Place subdivision

Indicators	1		Blank
	2		Non-filing characters
		0-9	- Number of non-filing characters present

Examples	151	Ø0	$aBarcoo River (Qld. and S. Aust.)
	451	Ø0	$aCoopers Creek (Qld. and S. Aust.)
	151	Ø0	$aUrsa Major
	451	Ø0	$aDipper (Constellation)
	151	Ø0	$aAdirondack Mountains (N.Y.)
	451	Ø0	$aAdirondacks (N.Y.)

See Also from Tracing

The headings in the 5XX fields are see also tracings from an alternative heading to an established heading in the 1XX field of the record. Headings in the 5XX fields will normally be ones that are established in the 1XX field of another authority record.

With the structure that is established in MARC authority records it is not possible to have "blind" see also references, that is, a reference which leads the user *to* another heading which has no titles associated with it. By definition of the authority record, a heading in the 5XX fields will only occur in the online catalog if the corresponding 1XX heading has been used in a bibliographic record. It is possible, however, to have a see also reference *from* a heading that does not have any associated bibliographic records of its own. In this way if the user enters a heading which has not been used in the online catalog, they will be referred to an alternative heading.

If the relationship between the see also reference and the established heading is not clear, then a note may be added in one of the 6XX fields.

All the 5XX fields are repeatable as required.

500 R See Also From Tracing—Personal Name. This field is used to create a see also reference from an established personal name to the related established heading in the 1XX field of the current record.

Subfields	$a		Name (surnames and forenames)
	$q		Expansion of initials in parenthesis, i.e. a qualification of the name in fuller form
	$b		Number (roman numerals)
	$c	R	Titles or other words associated with name
	$d		Date

Indicators	1		Type of personal name

		0	- Forename
		1	- Single surname
		2	- Multiple surname
		3	- Name of the family

	2		Non-filing characters

		0-9	- Number of non-filing characters present

Examples	100	30	$aVan Horn family
	500	30	$aHorn family

110	20	$aCorinthian Hall (Kansas City, Mo.)
500	10	$aLong, Robert Alexander,$d1850-1934
		$xHomes and haunts$zMissouri

510 R See Also From Tracing—Corporate Name. This field contains a tracing for a corporate name "see also from reference." It is used to create a see also reference from an established meeting name to a related established heading in 110 field of the current record.

Subfields	$a		Name
	$b	R	Subheading (each subordinate unit in the hierarchy of the organization)
	$d	R	Date
	$c		Place
	$k		Form subheading

Indicators	1		Type of corporate name

		0	- Surname (inverted)
		1	- Place or place and name
		2	- Name (direct order)

	2		Non-filing characters

		0-9	- Number of non-filing characters present

Examples	110	10	$aMaryland.$bAir Management Administration
	510	10	$aMaryland.$bAir Quality Programs

511 R See Also From Tracing—Meeting Name. This field contains a tracing for a meeting name "see also from reference." It is used to create a see also reference from an established meeting name to a related established heading in field 111 of the current record.

Subfields	$a		Name of meeting or place element
	$q		Name if entry element ($a) under place
	$d		Date
	$c		Place
	$n		Number or designation
Indicators	1		Type of meeting name
		0	- Surname (inverted)
		1	- Place or place and name
		2	- Name (direct order)
	2		Non-filing characters
		0-9	- Number of non-filing characters present
Examples	111	20	$aInternational Drip Irrigation Congress
	511	20	$aInternational Drip Irrigation Meeting
	511	20	$aInternational Drip/Trickle Irrigation Congress

530 R See Also From Tracing—Uniform Title Heading. This field contains a tracing for a uniform title "see also from reference." It is used to create a see also reference from an established uniform title to a related established heading in field 130 of the current record.

Subfields	$a		Uniform title heading
	$p		Part or section
	$t		Title of the work
	$k		Form subheading
Indicators	1		Blank
	2		Non-filing characters
		0-9	- Number of characters ignored in filing
Examples	130	ƀ0	$aHabakkuk commentary
	530	ƀ0	$aDead Sea scrolls
	130	ƀ0	$aData report (Maryland. Air Management Administration)
	530	ƀ0	$aData report (Maryland. Air Quality Programs)

550 R See Also From Tracing—Topical Term. This field contains a tracing for a topical term "see also from reference." It is used to create a see also reference from an established topical subject heading to a related established heading in the 1XX field of the current record.

Subfields	$a		Topical subject heading
	$x	R	General subdivision
	$y	R	Period subdivision (chronological)
	$z	R	Place subdivision

Indicators	1		Blank
	2		Non-filing characters
		0-9	- Number of non-filing characters present

Examples	150	ⱓ0	$aMen actors
	550	ⱓ0	$aActors
	151	ⱓ0	$aCooper's Creek (Qld. and S.Aust.)
	550	ⱓ0	$aRivers$zAustralia
	150	ⱓ0	$aSand Creek, Battle of, 1864
	550	ⱓ0	$aIndians of North America$xWars$y1862-1865

Continuing the Eskimo/Inuit example, the *LCSH* library will include the following fields in authority record for "Eskimos":

	550	ⱓ0	$aArtic races
	550	ⱓ0	$aIndians of North America
	550	ⱓ0	$aAleuts
	550	ⱓ0	$aChugach Eskimos

and so on for all the see also from references related to this heading.

The Canadian library would have the following fields in the "Inuit—Canada" record:

	550	ⱓ0	$aIndians of North America$zCanada
	551	ⱓ0	$aCanada$xNative races

551 See Also From Tracing—Geographic Name. This field contains a tracing for a geographic name "see also from reference." It is used to create a see also reference from an established geographic name to a related established heading in a 1XX field of the current record.

Subfields	$a		Geographic name
	$x	R	General subdivision
	$y	R	Period subdivision (chronological)
	$z	R	Place subdivision

Indicators	1		Blank
	2		non-filing characters
			0-9 - number of non-filing characters present

Examples	151	ƀ0	$aChelsea (London, England)
	551	ƀ0	$aKensington and Chelsea (London, England)
	551	ƀ0	$aLondon (England)
	111	ƀ0	$aCentral Australian Gold Exploration Company Expedition$d(1930)
	551	ƀ0	$aAustralia$xExploring expeditions

Notes (600 Level)

Sometimes it is necessary to include notes in the authority record in order to indicate the source of information on which the established heading is based, or to clarify a relationship between headings. There are a wide variety of notes which can be included, two of the most useful and important are described below.

680 R Subject Scope Note. Field 680 is used for explanatory information about a 1XX subject heading. It may be used for information such as the scope and usage of similar headings, and notices to users. The information is intended for display in the public catalog as well as guiding catalogers.

Subfield	$i	R	Explanatory text
	$a	R	Subject heading used to amplify the explanatory text of the scope note

Indicators	Blank		

Example	100	10	$aShakespeare, William,$d1564-1616
	680	ƀƀ	$iThe subdivisions provided under this heading represent for the greater part standard subdivisions usable under any literary author heading and do not necessarily pertain to Shakespeare.
	150	ƀ0	$aFire-damp

680 ƀƀ $iHere are entered works on methane as a combustible gas formed in coal mines. Works on methane present in a stratum of coal are entered under $aCoalbed methane.

The brief outline to MARC authority records that is provided above is intended as an introduction to a complex process. We have simplified the record and not included some of the further capabilities that are provided through special codes for different kinds of references, and other fields (2XX and 3XX) for "complex" cross-references. Readers who are interested in further study of this topic should consult the USMARC and CANMARC authority manuals.

In general it is the research and resource libraries that use authorities to the fullest extent. This introduction was intended to present the principles of authority control and to provide an introduction to an important aspect of online catalog management. Many automated systems for smaller libraries provide limited authority control using the same principles of only storing the correct heading once and linking to bibliographic records that need to use that heading. As the distribution of MARC authority records becomes more widespread, we can expect these smaller systems to begin to provide the capability to load externally derived authority records as required. As with bibliographic records, we can expect MARC to be the standard for communicating these records and integrating them into a local library system.

Establishing Authority Control

The question of when to establish correct headings during a recon project is discussed in Chapter 5. Authority control is an important aspect of establishing standards for the online bibliographic database. If an external vendor is to be used to provide authority control after the bibliographic records have been created, then the fields to be matched must be defined, and the process is approximately as follows:

Select a vendor. The issues to be considered in selecting a vendor for providing authority records is discussed in Chapter 5. Selection will be based primarily on the files available from the vendor, the services offered, and the cost of processing your bibliographic files.

Establish parameters and hierarchy for the authority record-matching process. In consultation with the vendor you have to establish parameters for database work. If there is more than one authority source file available for processing, it is also necessary to establish a hierarchy of authority files against which your records will be validated. This means that an American library can choose to give priority to authority records from the Library of Congress or Blackwell North America, while a Canadian library can give priority to the bilingual National Library of Canada authority files. In validating the bibliographic headings the processing program will be guided by the hierarchy and check authority files in the order defined by the customer.

Send a copy of the bibliographic file to the selected vendor. Having established the parameters for database processing, the library creates or orders a copy of its bibliographic file in MARC format on magnetic tape. This is forwarded to the vendor for processing. If the recon project has been done by an outside vendor then this file may already be available at the vendor's processing site.

Vendor processes the bibliographic records against the authority files. In order to check each of the fields which are to be authority controlled, the vendor "normalizes" each heading in the record. Normalizing the heading means that all the punctuation and spacing is stripped from the heading and the remaining characters are capitalized so that they can be matched against the equivalent string of characters in the indexes.

For example, from the 100 field of the bibliographic record:

> Shakespeare, William, 1564-1616.

becomes

> SHAKESPEAREWILLIAM15641616

when normalized. This will match against the search key in the personal name index during processing. The same method is used for normalizing subject, uniform title, and series entries.

Bibliographic record fields could be matched or validated against authority record fields as follows:

Bibliographic Record Fields	Authority Record Established Headings and See From Tracings					
Main entries						
100 - Personal Name	100,	400				
110 - Corporate Name	110,	111,	151,	410,	411,	451
111 - Conference or Meeting	111,	411				
130 - Uniform Title	130,	430				
Title entries						
240 - Uniform Title	100,	110,	111,	400,	410,	411
Series entries (traced)						
440 - Title	130,	430				
Subject entries						
600 - Personal Name	100,	400				
610 - Corporate Name	110,	111,	151,	410,	411,	451
611 - Conference or Meeting	111,	411				
630 - Uniform Title	130,	430				
650 - Topical Subject	150,	450				
651 - Geographic Name	110,	151,	450,	451		

Bibliographic Record Fields	Authority Record Established Headings and See From Tracings			
Added entries				
700 - Personal Name	100,	400		
710 - Corporate Name	110,	151,	410,	451
711 - Conference or Meeting	111,	411		
730 - Uniform Title	130,	430		
Series added entries				
840 - Title or Uniform Title	130,	430		

If a match is made against the 1XX field of an authority record, then the heading in the bibliographic record is correct and the authority record is flagged for selection at the end of the process. If the bibliographic record heading matches against a 4XX field in the authority record, that means that the library is using a heading which is not correct. The authority control process "flips" the heading in the bibliographic record to the correct entry, which is in the 1XX field of the authority record, and flags the authority record for selection. The diagram below shows this process in a graphic form.

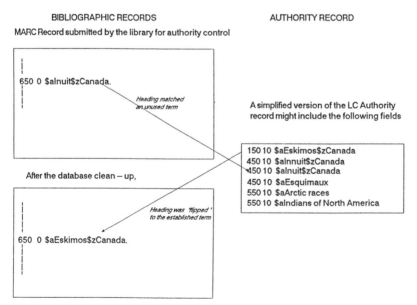

BIBLIOGRAPHIC RECORDS

MARC Record submitted by the library for authority control

650 0 $alnuit$zCanada.

Heading matched an unused term

AUTHORITY RECORD

A simplified version of the LC Authority record might include the following fields

150 10 $aEskimos$zCanada
450 10 $alnnuit$zCanada
450 10 $alnuit$zCanada
450 10 $aEsquimaux
550 10 $aArctic races
550 10 $alndians of North America

After the database clean – up,

650 0 $aEskimos$zCanada.

Heading was 'flipped' to the established term

If the library has set LC Subject authorities at the top of the validation hierarchy, then the heading in the submitted record will be 'flipped' to the established heading

From this description you can now see why it is so important for the vendor's authority files to be up-to-date and why the library should establish a hierarchy of preferred authority files for the matching process. Throughout this chapter we have used the example of the different headings used for Eskimos by Library of Congress and National Library of Canada. The U.S. library would establish *LCSH* authority records as the preferred source of authority control, whereas the Canadian library would choose National Library of Canada *CSH* as the top priority. In this way each library's database could be checked against the same authority files, but the library's preferences for matching can be accommodated.

The currency of the vendor's authority files is also critical. For example, in *LCSH* the heading for"Blacks" has changed over the years and in order to establish the most recent version of the heading in your bibliographic files and provide the correct cross-references the vendor's authority files must contain the latest version of all Library of Congress authority records.

Some vendors support the establishment of user authority records. These can be created by the library before database processing for any headings that are nonstandard in the bibliographic files, and which the library wishes to preserve. In order to preserve these headings, the user authority records must also be placed at the top of the validation hierarchy, and be checked before any other source files which might "flip" the bibliographic heading to another version.

Vendor creates bibliographic and authority record tapes for return to the library. After completing the processing of each bibliographic record in the library's file, the vendor creates two products for the library. The first is a file of MARC records on magnetic tape which represent the library's bibliographic records with the corrected, or "flipped," headings. The second product is a file of MARC authority records that were flagged during processing and correspond to the headings in the bibliographic records that found a match in the vendor's authority files. By loading these corresponding authority records the library will be able to establish consistent headings in its local database and provide the online catalog users with "see" and "see also" references.

Library loads bibliographic records and linked authority records. When the bibliographic and authority files arrive at the library, they have to be loaded into the local library system. Each automated system does this in slightly different ways. In general, the records are processed one by one, and as each record is loaded the appropriate search access points are created, and bibliographic and authority records are linked.

Different fields will be flagged for different search indexes. For example, the personal name headings from the 100, 600, and 700 fields will be indexed in the personal name index. The headings from the 110, 610, and 710 fields go into the corporate name index. Under the same principles, the 6XX headings will also go into the subject index. Individual words from some fields, such as the authors, titles, and subjects, will also be included in the keyword index. Most smaller library systems make no differentiation between main entry (1XX) fields and added entries (7XX), hence our earlier comment that main entry has less significance in an online environment.

Library maintains local authority files. Once the recon project is completed, and the library has implemented online cataloging, the authority files must be maintained by the catalogers. This means creating records manually based on the tools available, such as *LCSH*, or *Medical Subject Headings (MESH)* and incorporating changes and deletions as appropriate. An alternative to in-house creation of authority records is to derive them on an ongoing basis from a bibliographic utility or CD-ROM source.

In concluding this chapter on authority control, we would like to summarize the advantages and disadvantages of online authority control. The advantages of authority control are that:

- it maintains an established heading as a single entity and links all bibliographic records using that heading to the authority record
- a change to the authority record is "global" and reflected in all bibliographic records using that heading
- see and see also references can be maintained in the online catalog
- it improves the accuracy and relevance of online retrieval by collocating records under controlled headings
- storage of bibliographic information is more efficient and duplication of headings is reduced
- maintenance of controlled headings improves the consistency of printed products

The disadvantages are that:

- there is an added cost to the initial recon project for creating an authority file and establishing cross-references
- presently most authority control and maintenance on small local systems has to be derived from printed sources.

Having considered these advantages and disadvantages, you should be able to decide whether the cost justifies the effort involved.

Checklist:
MARC Authority Records

Leader   Information provided to the application program about how to process the record

Directory   Detailed information about the layout of the record

Variable length control fields

001   Control number

005   Date and Time of Latest Transaction

008   Fixed length data elements - general information

Variable length fields

010   Library of Congress Authority Control Number

040   Record Source

Established headings

100   Personal Name

110   Corporate Name

111   Conference or Meeting

130   Uniform Title

150   Topical Term

151   Geographic Name

See from tracings

400   Personal Name

410   Corporate Name

411   Conference or Meeting

430   Uniform Title

450   Topical Term

451   Geographic Name

See also from tracings

500   Personal Name

510   Corporate Name

511   Conference or Meeting

530   Uniform Title

550   Topical Term

551   Geographic Name

Notes

680   Subject Scope Note

Obtaining authority records and establishing control of headings

- Select a vendor or source of records
- Establish parameters and hierarchy for authority control
- Send a copy of the bibliographic file to the selected vendor
- Vendor processes the bibliographic records against the authority files
- Vendor creates tapes for return to the library
- Library loads bibliographic records and linked authority files
- Library maintains local authority files

Advantages of authority control:

- efficient storage of bibliographic information
- supports global changes to bibliographic records
- see and see also references can be maintained in the online catalog
- improves the accuracy and relevance of online retrieval
- controlled headings improve the consistency of printed products.

The disadvantages are:

- added cost to the initial recon project
- most authority records for small local systems are derived from printed sources

Further Reading

Bills, Linda G., and Linda W. Helgerson. "CD-ROM Public Access Catalogs: Database Creation and Maintenance." *Library Hi Tech* 6, no 1 (1988) : 67-86.

Library of Congress. Automation Planning and Liaison Office. *Authorities: A MARC Format*. Washington, DC: Library of Congress, 1981.

Library of Congress. Network Development and MARC Standards Office. *USMARC Authority Format Including Guidelines for Content Designation*. Washington, DC: Library of Congress, 1987- . Looseleaf. (Superintendent of Documents No. LC1.6/4:Au8)

Library of Congress. Subject Cataloging Division. Processing Services. *Library of Congress Subject Headings*. 11th Edition. Washington, DC: Library of Congress, 1988.

McDonald, David R. "MARC: the Foundation of Library Automation." *Journal of Academic Librarianship* 13 (July 1987): 168c-168d : insert between 168-69.

National Library of Canada. *Canadian Subject Headings*. 2d. Edition. Ottawa: 1985. (DSS cat. no. SN3-106/1985)

National Library of Canada. Canadian MARC Office. *Canadian MARC Communications Format: Authorities*. 3rd. Edition. Ottawa: National Library of Canada, 1988- . Looseleaf. (DSS cat. no. SN3-123/1988E)

13
Implementation and Project Management

In this chapter we will share our experiences in recon and the introduction of MARC to a library's cataloging process by providing some practical tips on the management of a recon project and the introduction of online cataloging to the library.

In the earlier chapters we discussed in detail the steps that need to be taken in deciding how to tackle the recon project. Once the decision has been made the real work begins!

The Recon Project

The importance of establishing a plan of action and preparing a procedures manual for staff involved in the recon was discussed in Chapter 9.

The tasks that we are describing here relate primarily to the details of doing an in-house recon project with a microcomputer. If an external vendor has been chosen to do recon then not all of these steps will be required.

Recruit staff. Based on the funds available and the staffing requirements that you have established, staff should be interviewed and hired. It is important to recruit staff who have appropriate skills or have shown an aptitude for learning to do accurate, routine work. The quality of the final product will depend to a great extent on the continued accuracy of operators over a long period of time.

Confirm timetable and task lists. With the staffing established it should be possible to confirm the timetable and task lists that had been previously drawn up.

Provide staff training. If staff need basic training in the use and management of microcomputers before starting the project, this should be arranged at the library or by sending staff to local courses. Other training, such as the library background information, coding shelf-list cards, use of software, and follow up editing and quality control, should be a mix of group and hands-on training. Training should be supplemented by the procedures manual, which describes the step-by-step conversion of catalog records.

Communicate regularly with staff and management. Throughout the project it is important to communicate regularly with the recon team regarding problems as they arise and general progress of the project. A barometer on the wall, similar to ones used in fund-raising projects, is a graphic way of telling the team and the rest of the library how the project is progressing.

Regular staff, who are not directly involved in the recon but will be affected by the change to online cataloging, should be kept informed throughout the project so that the advent of new technology in the library is not threatening.

Management should also be kept informed and alerted if serious delays or problems arise.

Establish procedures for control of shelf-list card batches. Regardless of the recon option that is chosen, it is important to keep track of all shelf-list cards and know exactly how many bibliographic records have been created. By knowing how many records are being loaded into the automated system, you can check that all the records have been loaded. Sampling of the loaded database is also necessary to check that the indexing is correct and records are retrievable.

The best way to keep track of records is to divide the shelf-list up into manageable batches of approximately 100 to 150 cards. Each batch is then recorded as it is given to an operator. For individual batch management, a colored 5x3-inch slip similar to the one shown below is very useful, since it can be placed on the top of each batch for control purposes.

BATCH # _____	DISKETTE # _____
SHELF-LIST RANGE	
START: _____	FINISH: _____
DATE	
START: _____	FINISH: _____
OPERATOR: _____	TOTAL RECORDS:_____
PROOF:_____ EDIT:_____	QUALITY CONTROL: ____

The example above assumes that records are being recorded on diskettes. This example can be adapted for other kinds of batch control, such as when records are being entered directly into the local library system or a utility database.

As the supervisor of the recon project assigns each batch to an operator, it should be logged on a master control sheet, something like the one shown below.

BATCH	START CALL#	FINISH CALL#	OPERATOR	START DATE	FINISH DATE	TOTAL RECORDS	DISK #

When batches are returned to the supervisor after the records have been proofread, edited, and sampled for quality control, the total records in the batch, and the diskette on which the records are stored, should be noted.

If recon is being done using a microcomputer, each operator should be assigned diskettes in pairs. One diskette is the working copy on which all new records are stored. The second diskette is for backing up the working copy each day. At the end of a session the operator should immediately copy the working diskette to the back-up diskette. When a diskette is full, two back-ups should be made and at least one of them should be stored off-site and away from the library in case of fire or theft. Procedures with back-up tapes, if diskettes are not being used, should be the same. The library's database is the unique feature that customizes an automated system to meet a particular library's needs. Therefore it should be very carefully protected.

In the day-to-day operation of the recon project, the supervisor should monitor progress and make regular quality control checks on the work being done. Targets for each month, that have been agreed to by all members of the team, help to show that progress is being made and provide an incentive.

Proofreading, quality control, and follow-up. For quality control, fields that are critical to online retrieval and printed products should be selected for special attention. For example, the call number is critical to finding a book on the shelves, and the nonfiling indicator for titles ensures that the titles are indexed correctly and are retrievable. Other indexed fields, such as authors and subjects, should also be carefully proofread. Fields such as the notes, collation, and imprint are much less important and time should not be spent on checking these. Depending on how your recon team is organized, you may or may not find it convenient for operators to proofread each other's work.

Monitor progress. The recon supervisor should monitor progress against the agreed targets and be open to suggestions from the team about different ways to do things. As experience is gained, there will always be room for improvements to the procedures and for fine tuning. For example, you may be able to reduce proofreading if the team achieves a high level of accuracy.

Completing the project—tying up the loose ends. When the last shelf-list card has been processed, this is surely a time for celebration! However, there will be loose ends to tie up. After the records have been loaded, some clean-up projects to fix headings and information that was not controlled during the recon may be necessary. Many libraries have found that clean-up projects can take on a life of their own. There is a fine line between clean-up and day-to-day catalog maintenance which is now going to be done online. Recon staff often become the database maintenance staff in the newly automated environment.

There is much more that could be said about managing the recon project, which is beyond the scope of this book. The best sources of practical advice about recon projects are your colleagues who have already gone through the process. And when you have completed your catalog conversion, please, share your experiences.

Implementing MARC

Introducing MARC coding to the library for recon or ongoing cataloging involves radical changes in the practices of the catalogers. Ideally, catalogers should not have to be concerned with the niceties of MARC coding because it is primarily an internal machine format for the communication of cataloging records. In practice, if you decide to use one of the CD-ROM-based sources of cataloging records or obtain records from an external source, you have to be able to interpret the information that is being received. This is the reason why so many more librarians are being confronted with MARC at this time and a motivating factor in producing this book.

The following steps need to be taken to introduce MARC to your library.

Develop a profile of the fields to be used in your library. The first step in introducing MARC is to develop a profile of the fields to be used in your library. The fields described in Chapter 11 represent a reasonable level of coding that can be used to describe unique titles in the collection of small- and medium-sized libraries. It also should provide sufficient information for reporting to regional union catalogs, although it does not meet the official minimum level required by the national libraries.

The library's own practices should be maintained in a cataloger's coding manual. This manual may consist of annotated versions of the appropriate pages of a MARC manual or this book. Ideally, a single page should be maintained for each field that the library wishes to use.

This profile should be a guide to acceptable record content and format at your library. For each field that will be used, the tags, subfields, and indicators should be described. Default values for the indicators should also be highlighted. This profile should be developed, bearing in mind the level of detail that is supported by the automated system that will be managing these records. There is no point in defining very complex records if your system only loads and stores a minimal level record. For example, you will find that many of the small systems ignore all indicators except the nonfiling indicators.

In addition to the field description information, all codes and symbols that are used in the library for material types, locations, and collections should also be recorded.

Some fields may be mandatory in order to file a record, e.g., the title. If this is the case with your system, then this should be recorded in the coding manual.

Finally a copy of the valid MARC codes for country of publication and languages should be obtained and included in the manual.

Set validity checks where possible. Some automated systems support the use of validation techniques to check information in selected fields as the record is filed. One of the most common validation checks that is carried out is on the structure of the ISBN. Other validation checks will relate to the presence or absence of data, e.g., title or date of publication, formatting LCCNs based on the position of the hyphen, whether the field should have numeric or alpha characters only, and validating predefined library codes.

Establish procedures for rejects. If you are loading records obtained from an external source into your automated system, a process must be established for dealing with any records that are rejected during the batch-loading process. Records may be rejected for a variety of reasons—for example, invalid or missing data. Rejected records should be dumped into a reject file so that they can be reviewed and corrected before attempting to reload them.

Develop sampling mechanism for quality control. Completion of the loading process does not automatically mean that every record is now correctly loaded and retrievable. In order to ensure integrity of the catalog, it is essential to sample the database and maintain careful quality control after every load. Quality control procedures, like those developed for the recon project, should be detailed enough to sample the database consistently and check that the programs are operating as expected. At the start of the loading process, and after a new version of software has been introduced, it may be necessary to sample every tenth record. Sampling should involve searching specific records by every defined access point and ensuring that the correct record is retrieved and displayed. Once you are confident that the programs are working correctly every hundredth record may be sufficient for sampling. An alternative to sequential sampling is to select certain types or ranges of records and known problem records. It is useful to have printouts or cards for the records that are sampled so that you can check information displayed on the screen against a printed source.

Correct records with detected errors. Records that are dumped in the reject file during the batch-loading process need to be corrected and then reloaded. This will involve adding missing data, and correcting tags, codes, or subfield delimiters. Then the records can be included in the next database load.

It is important to remember that the computer is very good at detecting errors in predefined coding, such as tags and coded data in the fixed fields, but errors in bibliographic information itself cannot be identified by computer. The cataloger still has ultimate responsibility for the *content* of the cataloging record. Records that are created online must be proofread and corrected by operators as required.

We hope that you have been able to use this book as guide from start to finish of a recon project. We have tried to layout the logical sequence of events that must occur in tackling the conversion of a card catalog to machine-readable format:

Decide whether recon is appropriate for your library.

- Determine what are the library's specific needs for recon.
- Establish standards and parameters for the project.
- Identify and analyze the recon options.
- Choose the best option for your situation.
- Develop an action plan for the recon project.

To supplement these guidelines, we have also provided the basic information that is necessary for actually doing the recon:

- Coding for MARC bibliographic records.
- Coding for MARC authority records.

This chapter was intended to provide some practical tips on handling the recon if you decide to do it in-house, and on managing the loading of records derived from elsewhere. The final chapter provides some guidelines for editing derived records.

Checklist:
Implementation and Project Management

The Recon Project

- Recruit staff
- Confirm timetable and task lists
- Provide staff training
- Communicate regularly with staff and management
- Establish procedures for control of shelf-list card batches
- Proofreading, quality control and follow-up
- Monitor progress
- Complete the project and tie up loose ends

Implementing MARC

- Develop a profile of fields to be used
- Set validity checks where possible
- Develop sampling mechanism for quality control
- Correct records with detected errors

Further Reading

Merrett, C., and Colleen Vietzen. "Aspects of Card Catalogue Conversion at the University of Natal Library, Pietermaritzburg." *South African Journal of Library and Information Science* 53 (June 1985): 89-94.

Millican, Rita. "Serials Conversion: LSU's Experience." *Serials Librarian* 9 (Summer 1985): 45-51.

Smith, Sharon, Robert Watkins, and Shirley Richardson. "Retrospective Conversion of Serials at the University of Houston: Midterm Report." *Serials Librarian* 9 (Spring 1985): 63-68.

14
Editing Derived Records

Because of the problems and costs involved in editing in a recon project, it seems appropriate to discuss the matter in some detail. This chapter deals primarily with the editing of derived records, although it will also be of some benefit to those who have used the direct data entry method. It is likely that the records you derive from another database will not match exactly the records that you have in your manual file. The question arises as to whether or not you edit the records you derive. Editing is really a question of cost, access, and integrity of library files.

Cost. Be assured that every time you edit a record, you are increasing the per record cost of the recon project. There is staff time to consider, as well as computer resources, and perhaps in some cases, time-consuming changes to manual files, be they bibliographic or authority. One of the problems with editing costs is that they cannot be known in advance, because before you begin the editing process you really do not know the quantity of editing to be done. Editing can wreak havoc with a recon budget and ultimately cause the project to fail unless editing costs are controlled.

Access. On the other hand, the reason for editing records is to improve access to the bibliographic file, and there is, therefore, quite a payoff if the editing is done sensibly. It is of little use creating large numbers of machine-readable records if they create confusion for both library staff and users. One can improve access to the collection through editing by making headings conform to a standard, and by correct coding and transcription.

Integrity of files. Coupled with access is the issue of the integrity of the library catalog. A change in one part of the catalog can often necessitate a change in another. This is especially evident to those libraries that maintain "see also" references in their catalogs. An editing change in one record could mean a change in three other records, which is necessary if the overall objective of the file is to be maintained. The integrity of data in the file improves access for library users but can be a drain on recon resources.

Is there a solution to the editing dilemma? In the ideal library catalog created by a recon project, every heading would be established according to *AACR2*, with the most up-to-date subject headings used, with no typos or incorrect coding. In reality, of course, such a catalog is very difficult and expensive to create. The real situation necessitates compromises. Hence there will be both pre-*AACR2* and *AACR2* headings; there will be varieties of subject headings of different vintages; and some incorrect data will creep in. What is important from the point of view of a sucessful recon project is to know in advance what specific *types* of editing changes will be made and be prepared to change policies if necessary in order to finish the project. For instance, some libraries have begun recon projects with the idea of having all records in ISBD format. After the projects ground to a halt it became evident that such editing was inappropriate, did little to improve access to the specific library catalogs and collections, and had to be abandoned in favor of more useful editing policies.

Editing Decisions

Following are some guidelines for identifying editing problems in records derived or created during the recon project. Each individual library should decide which are applicable and develop editing policies which reflect its needs. The editing decisions you will have to make will fall into the following categories.

Coding. It is important for subsequent retrieval that the coding in the records you derive or enter originally be correct. For instance, in the title field it is important that the indicators be set to the correct values so that the title will either be traced or untraced, or that the correct number of spaces be ignored for filing purposes. (A fuller discussion of this appears in the sections on MARC, Chapters 10–12.) Depending on the size of the recon project, it may not be feasible to check each and every field in each and every record, so you will probably want to sample records to make sure that there are not many errors. At the beginning of the project, you will want to check perhaps one in every ten records and then as you identify and solve any problems, you may want to check one out of every hundred records.

Transcription. The data from the cards should be entered correctly and the data in derived records should be correct. In an online catalog there is little tolerance for typographical errors and so typos can cause a record to be irretrievable. It should be noted that the direct data entry method of recon increases the possibility of finding typos in the records, more than if the records are derived from a national library. For example "Dump tricks" instead of "Dump trucks" in a subject heading will mean that in a keyword subject search, the user searching for "TRUCKS" will miss at least one reference and the user searching for "TRICKS" will get at least one very strange reference.

Punctuation and spacing. Each individual library has to decide what is important in punctuation. If the records are being entered directly from the shelf-list cards, it is relatively simple to add ISBD puntuation. If, however, the records are being derived, and ISBD is not present in the records (which is often the case), then you will have to decide on its importance. It will take time and effort, though, to add such punctuation.

More data or less data. It is often the case that derived records will have either more bibliographic information or less bibliographic information than what you have decided is necessary for your catalog. It is important that you know before the project begins what the minimum data elements will be in the records in your database. This means in a MARC record identifying the fixed and variable fields you need as a minimum, and deciding on the level of subject access to be provided.

If you are doing recon by the direct data entry method and the shelf-list cards do not contain all the information you want, then decide if you need to upgrade the records. Be aware of the time and cost implications of such a move. The same will apply if you are deriving records from an external source. You may wish to add data to the derived record if it does not meet your standards.

On the other hand, it is possible that the records you derive will contain more information than you consider necessary. If storage space is a concern you may wish to delete some information, although it can sometimes be the case that the cost of deletion of unwanted data is greater than its storage cost. Unless data has an adverse effect on your local system, it is probably not worth the time and effort to delete extra data.

Fixed fields. As stated previously, you must decide before the project begins what fixed fields you consider to be necessary for the records in your database. Once you have decided that, you may want to periodically check that the records you are acquiring contain those fixed fields. If they do not you should add them at the editing stage. If there are more fixed fields than you need, then you can probably leave them, although you should check with your local systems vendor.

Variable fields. For editing purposes the variable fields can be divided into nonindexed variable fields and indexed variable fields. Typically, nonindexed fields, those fields which are not access points to the bibliographic record and which cannot be searched on, such as the collation field (300 in the MARC record), or the notes fields (5XX), are not edited. You may want, however, to make sure that important notes contained on your shelf-list cards be entered into the machine-readable record.

The indexed variable fields present a much greater problem in that access to the bibliographic records and hence to your collection depends on the quality and completeness of the data in the indexed fields. It is in cleaning up headings in the indexed variable fields that the real headaches of editing begin. While it depends on the particular system that you are using, the fields of the machine-readable record which are typically indexed are the names, titles, series, and subjects fields, and some systems will also allow you to use the information in the publication information field and the edition statement field to qualify a search.

Names, titles, and subjects. From an access point of view, in a machine-readable file the most important fields are the names, titles, and subjects fields, which, as in the card catalog, are the most frequently searched fields. It is obvious that the main title field should match the title on the item in your collection or the title on the shelf-list card. Some brief, machine-readable records which you derive may not have "other title information" in the record and so a decision will be made whether or not to accept these records as is or to add the other title information which appears on your shelf-list cards. For the most part, libraries choose to accept these records as is and not add the extra title information.

Other headings, such as names, subjects, and some series, present other problems which must be resolved. Unlike a card catalog where similar headings can be interfiled and treated as if they were the same, in the online catalog every heading is filed exactly as it is in the record and hence similar headings can be dispersed throughout the file and cause problems for retrieval. (Examples and solutions for these problems are described in the authorities section, Chapter 12). The problem from an editing point of view is that when you are deriving records from an outside source, the headings in the records which you derive may not necessarily match those in your own machine-readable file or even match other records in the file from which you are deriving.

You must decide, therefore, whether or not you are going to make sure the headings in your machine-readable file have some kind of authority control mechanism and if you are going to edit the derived records so that various forms of the same name are standardized to one single form. If you are using the direct data entry method, you will have to determine if the headings on the shelf-list cards are standardized and can be input exactly as found on the cards or if some editing will have to be done to the headings.

Choices

After having identified for your library what the editing problems are, you are now in a position to decide how and when to tackle the editing task. In regards to headings, you have four fundamental choices when dealing with derived records.

• **Accept whatever is found in the derived record.** In this case no editing changes are made to the records. You accept whatever appears on the derived record, even if it is different than the information on the shelf-list card. This may be fine if the record is from a national agency and the database from which it is derived is under authority control. If neither of those conditions is satisfied, you can expect to have access problems in the future if you do no editing to the records.

• **Make headings in the derived record match the manual record.** In this case you are assuming that the headings in the manual file are standardized, and that by making the headings in the derived records match the records in the manual file that you are going to have a file free of conflicts. If this assumption—that is, that there are various forms of the same name (for example, pre-*AACR2* and *AACR2* headings) in the manual file—is not correct, then you may not achieve very much by the editing process, as you will still have conflicting headings in your machine-readable file.

• **Make changes when it avoids or resolves a conflict.** In this case the objective is to maintain a machine-readable file which is free of conflicts. It does not mean that every heading needs to be in *AACR2* form. There may well be older headings in the file which would be established differently under *AACR2*. What is important is that there is not a mix of forms of headings for the same name. In order to achieve this, for some headings you will accept whatever appears in the derived record, while for others you may change them to the form of heading found in the manual record. The use of this method presupposes that you have an authority file of headings used in the catalog.

• **Run the new file against a machine-readable authority file.** In this case, rather than editing each record separately, the newly created machine-readable file is machine matched against an authority file, usually containing at least *Library of Congress Name Authorities*. In this way headings can be changed to an authoritative form if necessary and many other conflicts are frequently identified for manual changes. Needless to say there is a cost for this service, which should be allowed for before the project begins. Be aware, too, that not every conflict will be resolved using this method. There will probably be a lot of manual clean-up to be done before all access problems will be resolved.

When to Do Editing

There are some choices as to when the editing of records can be done. Each library will have to decide when it is most approriate to do any editing, depending on personnel and resources. It can also depend on whether you use the direct data entry method or whether you derive the records. If you use direct data entry, you may wish to edit: before data entry; during data entry or deriving process; or after data entry or deriving process.

Before data entry. In this case you check the data on the shelf-list cards before you enter it into the system. If the data are incomplete, this is the time to enhance the bibliographic record if the standards you have adopted necessitate it. If the manual file is not already under authority control, it is possible to check headings against an authority file, although it would be time consuming and could be costly. This is also the time when coding, notes, etc., can be added to the shelf-list for the use of the data entry people.

During data entry or deriving process. Whether you are using the direct data entry method or deriving records from another file, you can edit the records as you go. If entering the records directly, then the terminal operators make changes to the manual shelf-list as the data are entered, following prescribed policies and procedures as laid out in a manual. If you are deriving records, then the records are checked and updated as soon as they arrive in the library or are filed with a bibliographic utility.

After data entry or deriving process. In this case all editing is left until the database is created and then a clean-up period follows. As stated previously, this process may involve running the database against an automated authority file, or it can mean looking at and editing each record separately. If the initial objective of the recon project is to create a file for circulation purposes, then many libraries get as many records converted and then worry about editing when the prospect of an online catalog appears. If, on the other hand, the objective is to create, from the outset, a file for an online catalog, then editing may have to be begun before the whole file is converted.

Conclusion

As with so many other decisions in the recon project, the decisions with regard to editing must be made locally and reflect the needs of the library. There are some difficult choices to make and this chapter can only identify the general problems and offer some general solutions. Let us stress again, however, that the heart of any automated library system is the database, and the better the database, the better the access will be to the library's collection.

We hope that this manual will provide you with the essential checklist for a recon project. If you are unsure about whether your library needs to do a recon, or how to start one, start looking at the options and use this book as your guide to resources and the questions that need to be asked. If you have already begun a recon, then keep this manual handy for checking your progress. When the recon is finally over, we also hope you will find the chapters on MARC a useful guide to ongoing coding and practices.

Good luck!

Checklist:
Editing Derived Records

Editing Decisions

- Coding
- Transcription
- Punctuation and spacing
- More data or less data
- Fixed fields
- Variable fields
- Names, titles, subjects

Choices

- Accept whatever is found in derived record
- Make everything in derived record match manual record
- Make changes when it avoids or resolves a conflict
- Run new file against a machine-readable authority file

When to Edit

- Before data entry
- During data entry or deriving process
- After data entry or deriving process

Further Reading

Boss, Richard W. *Issues in Retrospective Conversion.* N.p.: R.W. Boss, 1985.

Crismond, Linda F. "Quality Issues in Retrospective Conversion Projects." *Library Resources & Technical Services* 25 (January-March 1981): 48-55.

Gregor, Dorothy, comp. and ed. *Retrospective Conversion of Music Materials: Report of a Meeting Sponsored by the Council on Library Resources, July 18-19, 1984, Wayzata, Minnesota.* Washington, DC: Bibliographic Service Development Program, Council on Library Resources, 1984.

Johnson, Carolyn A. "Retrospective Conversion of Three Library Collections." *Information Technology and Libraries* 1 (June 1982): 133-39.

Juneja, Derry C. "Quality Control in Data Conversion." *Library Resources & Technical Services* 31 (April-June 1987): 148-58.

Kaplan, Denise P. "Creating Copy Specific Records for Local Databases." *Library Hi Tech* 2, no. 3 (1984): 19-24.

Kruger, Kathleen Joyce. "MARC Tags and Retrospective Conversion: The Editing Process." *Information Technology and Libraries* 4 (March 1985): 53-57.

Appendix I
Sources of MARC Records and Recon Services

The following information is compiled from literature provided by the vendors in response to requests made to them in 1988. The information has generally been transcribed as provided by the vendors and is intended simply as a guide to the types of services that vendors offer. The full names and addresses of the vendors are listed in Appendix II, and vendors should be contacted directly for more current information.

BLACKWELL NORTH AMERICA

Products and reports	Offers authority control services only; has cooperative arrangements with AMIGOS Bibliographic Council and OCLC, Inc. for retrospective conversion services

BRODART COMPANY

Interactive Access System

Hardware	Telex or IBM terminal, phone lines, modem; personal computer with emulator board; or personal computer without emulator board for dial access
Software	None needed for direct line access; conversion is completed via direct access to the Brodart computer facility; dial-up access requires emulator software
Database	MARC, MARC-Retro, Brodart-Retro, CANMARC, GPO, and a selection of individual libraries' databases
Access	LCCN, ISBN, author, title, subject

Products and reports	Ongoing database maintenance on IAS; database copy in machine-readable format; catalog on microfiche, microfilm or compact disc; public access to online file is also available
	No reports required; may produce shelf list cards and labels locally
Costs	Call Brodart Automation at 1-800-233-8467 ext. 640 (east), 1-800-643-0523 (west), or 1-800-821-1117 (California) for price quotes

Microcheck

Hardware	IBM PC compatible or Apple IIe, IIc, II+ with 128K memory
Software	PC-DOS or MS-DOS (IBM), PRO-DOS (Apple), MicroCheck
Database	MicroCheck is a batch oriented system; there are no resident databases; the LCMARC database on microfiche is a desirable aid but not required
Access	LCCN (preferred) or ISBN or short author/title
Products and reports	Database copy on magnetic tape; catalog on microfilm, microfiche, or compact disc
	Reports: error listings of unacceptable (not able to be processed) records are available
Costs	Call Brodart Automation at 1-800-233-8467 ext. 640 (east), 1-800-643-0523 (west), or 1-800-821-1117 (California) for price quotes

MITINET

Hardware	IBM PC compatible, 128K memory
Software	PC-DOS or MS-DOS, MITINET software
Database	MITINET is a batch-oriented system; there are no resident databases, however, the LCMARC database on microfiche is required

Access	LCCN and check digit
Products and reports	Database copy in machine-readable format; catalog on microfilm, microfiche, or compact disc
	Reports: error listings of unacceptable (not able to be processed) records are available throughout the conversion
Costs	Call Brodart Automation at 1-800-233-8467 ext. 640 (east), 1-800-643-0523 (west), or 1-800-821-1117 (California) for price quotes

Vendor Conversion Services

Hardware	None, as conversion is done at vendor site
Software	None, as conversion is done at vendor site
Database	MARC, MARC-Retro, Brodart-Retro, CANMARC, GPO and a selection of individual libraries' databases
Access	LCCN, ISBN, author, title, subject
Products and reports	Database copy in machine-readable format; catalog on microfiche, microfilm, or compact disc
	Ongoing status reports available for large collections
Costs	Call Brodart Automation at 1-800-233-8467 ext. 640 (east), 1-800-643-0523 (west), or 1-800-821-1117 (California) for price quotes

THE COMPUTER COMPANY

Bibliographic Data Management System (BDMS)

Hardware	IBM PC or compatible
Database	MARC sources include OCLC, RLIN, WLN and commercial firms
Products and reports	Copies of libraries' databases on magnetic tapes provided: USMARC II records, 1600 bpi or 6250 bpi, 9-track, ASCII, blocked to either Library of Congress Tape Specifications or OCLC Tape Specifications

Costs	$1.00 per title: TCC site, on-line conversion $.60 per title: Library site, on-line conversion $.18 per title: Tape conversion

EKI INCORPORATED

Search key service

Hardware	None
Software	None
Database	None
Access	Creates brief search records for matching against database of customer's choice
Products and reports	Brief search records
Costs	Custom conversion so conditions and prices are variable

Database creation service

Hardware	None
Software	None
Database	None
Access	Creates full MARC records
Products and reports	Full MARC records
Costs	Custom conversion so conditions and prices are variable

GAYLORD INFORMATION SYSTEMS

SPECTRUM SuperCAT

Hardware	Gaylord Information Systems ADD PC or ADD PC+, or equivalent IBM compatible; CD-players; Okidata 292 printer or equivalent is optional

Software	SPECTRUM SuperCAT cataloging software: includes software needed to edit LCMARC catalog records to fit local requirements; create original cataloging records; print edit sheets, catalog cards, spine labels, orders; retrieve and reuse local catalog records
	SuperCAT software may also be used with local files, e.g., union catalog files, mastered to optical or compact disc for the SPECTRUM 1000 ILL system or for other local files mastered by Gaylord Information Systems for SuperCAT
Database	LCMARC cataloging (MARC Distribution Service): Books, Serials, Visual Materials, Music, Maps; base subscription includes English-language records in all formats, with foreign-language records on a supplementary subscription
	Records are initially stored in Internal Processing Format (IPF), fully reconvertible to OCLC MARC format (software to reconvert included)
Access	LCCN, ISBN, ISSN, author (with or without title qualifier), title (with or without author qualifier)
Products and reports	Basic produce: machine-readable cataloging record, saved to floppy diskette or hard disk
	Optional products: catalog cards, spine/pocket labels, BISAC-format order
Costs	Upon request

GENERAL RESEARCH CORPORATION

LaserQuest

Hardware	IBM PC or compatible, MS-DOS or PC-DOS 512K memory, one diskette drive, Hitachi CD-ROM disc drive, modem optional
Software	Access software

Database	GRC's Database of more than 5 million MARC records (over 2 million contributed by GRC's accounts which include public libraries, universities, community colleges, public schools and special libraries from all over U.S. and Canada); 325,000 CANMARC Book and Music records
Access	Title, ISSN
Products and reports	Reworks can be saved to diskette; system can be linked to some circulation and online systems; can create a database at GRC; can produce CD-ROM or COM catalogs; catalog cards may be printed from records saved on diskettes; card sorting option, spine label printing available
Costs	Prices quoted upon request

INFORMATION TRANSFORM INC.

MITINET/retro

Hardware	IBM PC, XT, AT or compatible, 1 floppy disk drive; Apple IIe, IIc, 1 floppy disk drive
Software	For IBM PC: PC-DOS or MS-DOS For Apple II: DOS 3.3
Database	LCMARC file; contributed MARC titles from other MITINET users (primarily school library A/V titles)
Access	Access is by a unique MITINET match number (which includes a built-in check digit to prevent all types of keying errors) copied from a microfiche file, and entered on the micro screen. The 8-10 digit match number eliminates the need to enter any title, publisher, date, and author data
Products and reports	Single library or union catalog data bases in the LCMARC format; COM catalogs (microfilm or microfiche catalogs); CD-ROM catalogs (all services provided by Brodart Company) No reports generated
Costs	$250

THE LIBRARY CORPORATION

BiblioFile

Hardware	IBM PC or compatible, with 512K RAM and Hitachi CD-ROM drive 5 1/4" CD-ROM disks, 1 or 2 disk drives with interface to handle transmission to local system Optional: use with file server to mainframe system; printer (library supplied)
Software	Retrieval; display, edit, add local data; some validation warnings; store record on hard or floppy disk; create original records
Database	LCMARC: English on 2 disks, foreign on another; Books and Serials
Access	LCCN, ISBN, ISSN, GPO, author/title or title key May qualify by language, year or pagination
Products and reports	MARC records for local system or OCLC/MARC tape; CD-ROM library catalog; Cards, labels, edit sheets
Costs	Monthly or quarterly updates: $1,470 English monthly; $870 English quarterly; $500 foreign quarterly; $2,930 for CD-ROM drive and software. Further information available upon request

LIBRARY OF CONGRESS CATALOGING DISTRIBUTION SERVICE, PROCESSING SERVICES

Select MARC

Hardware	Tape loading facilities to process returned tapes
Software	No specific software needed
Database	Books, Serials, Maps, Music, and Visual Materials. The databases used for Select MARC are updated every day and represent the current status of Library of Congress cataloging

Access	LCCN, ISBN, or ISSN
Products and reports	Tapes containing records found; printout of the LCCNs found; separate tape and printed list of LCCNs not found; all records are distributed in standard USMARC format; UNIMARC output is available upon request
	Serial records include an 850 holding field
	Unable to add customer-supplied holdings data
Costs	$300 base fee per order + per record hit charge: orders submitted on 9-track tape, output costs $0.01 per record; orders submitted on floppy disk, output costs $0.02 per record; orders submitted in a hard copy medium, output costs $0.08 per record
	No charge for searches which do not produce records for the user

LIBRARY SYSTEMS AND SERVICES INC. (LSSI)

MINI MARC

Hardware	IBM PC (library supplied)
	12" laser disks, 2 disk drives, and controller
	Optional: 2 additional drives, multi-PC controller for up to 6 PCs, interface to local system; printers (library supplied)
Software	Retrieval; display, edit, add local data; minimal edit validation on filing; store record on hard or floppy disk; create original records; store REMARC key for no-hits; transfer records to another system
Database	LCMARC (2.1M records on 2 disks) English & Foreign books and serials; USGPO, LCMARC Films, Music, and Maps; NICEM - non-print materials; LCAUTH and CANMARC are under consideration
Access	LCCN, author/title key (OCLC); ISBN under development

Products and reports	MARC records; Cards, spine labels
Costs	Quarterly or biweekly updates: $4,800 biweekly, $1,600 quarterly Equipment: $17,975 for basic system

MITINET/marc

Hardware	IBM PC, XT, AT or compatible, 2 floppy disk drives, or 1 disk drive and a hard disk; Apple IIe, IIc, 2 floppy disk drives, or 1 disk drive and a hard disk
Software	For IBM PC: PC-DOS or MS-DOS For Apple II: ProDOS
Database	No database accessible
Access	By user assigned record number
Products and reports	USMARC records in the MARC communications format, stored on the user's floppy disk or hard drive Reports: 1) Bib Card Report (catalog records printed in a catalog card-like format, without MARC tagging) 2) MARC Print Report (catalog records printed in a MARC tagged format)
Costs	$495

MARCIVE

Hardware	Intelligent terminal, e.g., IBM PC and modem
Software	No special MARCIVE software; user creates files of keys with word processor or from within library system such as Sydney Requires communications software that supports file transfer Cataloging Input System (CIS) software
Database	LCMARC, USGPO, NLM, CANMARC

Access	LCCN, ISBN, NLM, NLC, GPO, i.e., numeric keys to various fields
Products and reports	Magnetic tape; records directly downloaded to local system; diskettes; COM or CD-ROM catalog; reports on number of hits and no-hits
Costs	Available upon request

NATIONAL LIBRARY OF CANADA

<u>Selected Records</u>

Hardware	For tape: tape drive
	For file transfer: disk drive
Software	Tape: conversion software from CANMARC format to internal format (not provided by NLC)
	File transfer: as above plus implementation of the file transfer protocol; communications software
Database	Canadiana Monographs, Canadiana Music and Sound Recordings, LCMARC, UKMARC, CONSER, Bibliotheque nationale (France)
Access	ISBN, ISSN, LCCN, Canadiana control number, OCLC no., title, author/title
Products and reports	Magnetic tape of MARC records
	Reports of records found/not found; statistical summary report; listing by title of records found
Costs	tape: $25.65/submission $.09/record file transfer: $25.65/submission $.17/record

<u>Retrospective Cumulations</u>

Hardware	Tape drive

Software	Conversion software from CANMARC communication format to internal format (not provided by NLC)
Database	Canadiana Monographs, Canadiana Music and Sound Recordings, LCMARC, UKMARC, CONSER, Bibliotheque nationale (France)
Access	By dates of coverage; by database
Products and reports	Magnetic tape of MARC records
	No reports
Costs	$440/submission $15.50/tape $0.006/record

Canadiana Monographs Tape Service

Hardware	Tape drive
Software	Conversion software from CANMARC communication format to internal format (not provided by NLC)
Database	Canadiana Monographs
Access	Weekly subscription tape
Products and reports	Weekly magnetic tape of MARC records
	Control number listing of records on tape
Costs	$595/year

Canadiana Music and Sound Recordings Tape Service

Hardware	Tape drive
Software	Conversion software from CANMARC communication format to internal format (not provided by NLC)
Database	Canadiana Music and Sound Recordings
Access	Monthly subscription tape

Products and reports	Monthly magnetic tape of MARC records
	Control number listing of records on tape
Costs	$395/year

LCMARC Tape Service

Hardware	Tape drive
Software	Conversion software from CANMARC communication format to internal format (not provided by NLC)
Database	LCMARC
Access	Weekly subscription tape
Products and reports	Weekly magnetic tape of MARC records control number listing of records on tape
Costs	$2,455/year

UKMARC Tape Service

Hardware	Tape drive
Software	Conversion software from CANMARC communication format to internal format (not provided by NLC)
Database	UKMARC
Access	Weekly subscription tape
Products and reports	Weekly magnetic tape of MARC records
	control number listing of records on tape
Costs	$1,530/year

CONSER Tape Service

Hardware	Tape drive
Software	Conversion software from CANMARC communication format to internal format (not provided by NLC)

Database	CONSER
Access	Subscription tape every four weeks
Products and reports	Magnetic tape of MARC records every four weeks
	No reports
Costs	$375/year

Bibliotheque Nationale (France) Tape Service

Hardware	Tape drive
Software	Conversion software from CANMARC communication format to internal format (not provided by NLC)
Database	Bibliotheque nationale (France)
Access	Monthly subscription tape
Products and reports	Monthly magnetic tape of MARC records
	control number listing of records on tape
Costs	$340/year

OCLC, Inc.

MICROCON

Hardware	M300 terminal or IBM PC compatible
Software	MICROCON software provided by OCLC; for IBM PC or compatible, DOS 2.0 or higher is needed
Database	Source and user contributed records: books, serials, A/V, manuscripts, maps, scores, sound recordings, etc. (OCLC Online Union Catalog has over 17 million records)
Access	OCLC control number, LCCN including prefixes, ISBN, ISSN, CODEN, MPN (Music Publisher Number), GDN (Government Document Number); personal name/title key or title key including qualifiers (format, imprint)

Products and reports	Magnetic tapes; holdings added to union catalog
	Exception reports listing: 2-10 hits; over 10 hits; no-hits
Costs	User pays only for single hits, approx. $.40/hit incl. tape product

MICROCON*PRO

Hardware	None
Software	None
Database	This service provides conversion using the entire OCLC Online Union Catalog of over 17 million records with more than 260 million holdings
Access	The MICROCON portion of this service provides a machine match of the following search keys: OCLC Control Number, LCCN, ISBN, ISSN, MPN (Music Publisher Number), CODEN, personal name/title, and title; all search keys except the unique OCLC control number may be qualified by publication date, format, and microform/not microform
	This multiple-hit and no-hit resolution option of this service involves operator searching and selection of the appropriate records
Products and reports	Output tape is an OCLC MARC tape in full MARC format for matching records. If original input is performed, the records input are on a separate tape from those converted through the MICROCON Service. Local data, such as holding information, call number and notes are merged into matching records
	Libraries wishing to perform their own multiple-hit and no-hit resolution may receive the standard MICROCON exception reports
	Reports: exception reports listing "2 - 10 Hits", "Over 10 Hits", and "No Hits." These exception reports are normally returned to the MICROCON*PRO staff for further processing; monthly updates

Costs	Costs are based on a "per record processed" basis. Each project is negotiated individually, according to requirements, with the average cost in the $.85 per record processed range. There is no charge for the MARC tape which results from the MICROCON conversion. The charge for the MARC tape on which original input is placed varies, depending on the regional network which provides the MARC tape subscription. MICROCON*PRO is available to both OCLC members and non-members. Minimal profiling is necessary for non-members

<u>TAPECON</u>

Hardware	Libraries will use that hardware which is required for them to format their existing tapes into the prescribed format for TAPECON processing
Software	Libraries will use that software which is required for them to format their existing tapes into the prescribed format for TAPECON processing
Database	This service provides a machine match of submitted search keys against the entire OCLC Online Union Catalog of over 17 million records with more than 260 million holdings.
Access	Formatted tapes are submitted for machine matching against the Online Union Catalog. Search keys accepted are: OCLC Control Number, LCCN, ISBN, ISSN, MPN (Music Publisher Number), GDN (Government Document Number), personal name/title, and title
	All search keys except the unique OCLC control number may be qualified by publication date, format, and microform/not microform
Products and reports	Output tape: OCLC MARC tape; local data merged into matching records
	Exception report lists search keys which resulted in multiple or no-hits. For multiple hits in the "2-10 Hits" category, a list of abbreviated records is provided from which the appropriate record may be chosen for re-entry on another TAPECON tape or through MICROCON. Search keys resulting in "Over 10 Hits" or "No Hits" are listed so that an alternative means of conversion may be used for these items.

Costs	Costs are based on a fixed rate for each record converted. Costs vary between $.34 and $.42 per single record converted. TAPECON is available to both OCLC members and non-members

RETROCON

Hardware	None
Software	None
Database	This service provides conversion against the entire OCLC Online Union Catalog of over 17 million records with more than 260 million holdings
Access	Search Online Union Catalog using detailed match specifications written in conjunction with the individual library
Products and reports	OCLC MARC tape in full MARC format for all records; local data merged into matching records
	Monthly reports
Costs	Can be less that $1.00 per title; available to OCLC members and non-members

Online retrospective conversion

Hardware	OCLC workstation or any IBM PC compatible computer with a modem
Software	OCLC Terminal Software is required for use of an OCLC workstation and recommended for use with an IBM PC compatible computer
Database	This service provides conversion using the entire OCLC Online Union Catalog of over 17 million records
Access	Database is searched using a variety of search keys, including OCLC Control Number, ISBN, ISSN, MPN (Music Publisher Number), GDN (Government Document Number), CODEN, personal name/title, and title

Products and reports	Output tape is an OCLC MARC tape in full MARC format; local data are added to matching records or included in original input
	Monthly report of system use is distributed in the form of a monthly billing statement
Costs	Costs vary according to the regional network which provides the service

ONTARIO LIBRARY SERVICES CENTER

LSC Bibliographic Data Base Conversion Services

Hardware	Microcomputer (IBM PC compatible) with at least 512K memory
Software	MS-DOS (version 2.1 or later); LSC provides other software
Database	LSC Acquisitions and/or Cataloging Data Bases; can also access National Library of Canada database
Access	LSC primarily uses ISBN search key
Products and reports	Print verification reports, magnetic tape, floppy diskettes and/or cartridges
Costs	By quotation

RESEARCH LIBRARIES GROUP, INC.

RLIN

Hardware	Any MS-DOS or PC-DOS computer with 80-character display and either two 5.25" floppy diskette drives or one diskette drive and one hard disk; PCs used to transmit files must have modems
	RPCON will extend the use of RLIN for retrospective conversion through batch searching and record derivation
Software	Provided by RLIN

Database	Includes many of the materials held by the members of the Research Libraries Group, Inc., as well as LC, USGPO, CONSER, NLM, and BNB
Access	Each search must include at least one of: title phrase, LCCN, ISBN, ISSN, RLIN ID and at least one more of the items above or edition, place of publication, publisher identification, date of publication
Products and reports	Tapes and cards; derived records become standard RLIN records
	Reports prepared for each file include a single-result log, an exception log, a small-result log and a combined no-result/large-result log. All reports are in search-ID order and include the contents of each search
Costs	Available upon request

SAZTEC

<u>Search key service</u>

Hardware	None
Software	None
Database	None
Access	Creates brief search arguments for matching against the UTLAS database, the B/NA database, or the Select MARC database of LC
Products and reports	MARC records available on magnetic tape
Costs	By quotation

<u>Tag and Key Service</u>

Hardware	None
Software	None
Database	None

Access	Creates full MARC format databases
Products and reports	Converts records from printed documents; creates mnemonic tags for authors, titles, dates, publishers, etc. for the local system; produces patron databases from printed source documents
Costs	Prices vary with the volume of data, the condition of the source documents, the local data conventions, the custom development required to implement the project

SOUTHEASTERN LIBRARY NETWORK INC.

SOLINET Laser Lease System

Hardware	PC systems including videodisc players, player controller, multihost controller and PC network interface boards
Software	Access software provided by SOLINET
Database	For libraries which are members of OCLC, a portion of the retrospective conversion project may be performed on the OCLC database (containing about 17 million records and including the LCMARC bibliographic file). Since numerous retrospective conversion projects have been performed using this system and database, it includes many records which date prior to the inception of LCMARC bibliographic records in 1968
Access	LCCN, ISBN, ISSN, title, author, control #
Products and reports	Full MARC record to magnetic tape, catalog cards, book labels; remastered on an annual basis
	No reports generated by system
Costs	Tape processing for transfer of data from floppy diskette to magnetic tape: job set-up: $25.00 processing (est. 350 records/diskette): $1.00/diskette record/check /analysis: $.0005 record tape charge: $25.00/tape shipping and handling: $5.00/tape

ReCon Service

Hardware	None
Software	None
Database	OCLC Online Union Catalog database and SOLINET database
Access	LCCN, ISBN, ISSN, title, author, control #
Products and reports	Full MARC record to magnetic tape, catalog cards, book labels
	No reports generated
Costs	Available upon request

UTLAS INTERNATIONAL

CATSS Online

Hardware	ASCII terminal or microcomputer operating in that mode; modem
Software	Utlas supplied software
Database	User contributed records; source records: LCMARC, UKMARC, CANMARC, INTERMARC, USGPO, NLM, etc.; LCMARC, CANMARC and user contributed authorities; over 40 million records
Access	Over 30 numeric and textual access points and full Boolean search capability
Products and reports	MARC tapes, cards, COM and a variety of book-form catalogs; full authority control available
Costs	Depend on system usage and include both connect time and transaction components

CATSSERVICES

Hardware	None, as all work done by Utlas' staff

Software	Utlas-supplied software
Database	User-contributed records; source records: LCMARC, UKMARC, CANMARC, INTERMARC, USGPO, NLM, etc.; LCMARC, CANMARC and user-contributed authorities; over 40 million records
Access	Over 30 numeric and textual access points and full Boolean search capability
Products and reports	MARC tapes, cards, COM and a variety of book-form catalogs; full authority control available
Costs	Depend on system usage and include both connect time and transaction components

M/Series 100 with DisCon

Hardware	IBM PC; 4 CD-ROM players
Software	Utlas provided
Database	4.2 million REMARC records and 1.8 LCMARC records (1968-84)
Access	LCCN, ISBN, ISSN, and title (including alternate and series). Search qualifiers are author, publisher, place and date of publication
Products and reports	MARC tapes, cards, COM and a variety of book-form catalogs; full authority control available
Costs	$1,200/month for 4 players and discs, software and documentation. Additional charge of $0.30 per record matched

M/Series 100 without DisCon

Hardware	IBM PC
Software	Utlas provided
Database	Full Utlas database
Access	Brief search keys: ISBN, LCCN, Ultas RSN

Products and reports	MARC tapes, cards, COM and a variety of book-form catalogs; full authority control available
Costs	$0.35-$0.60 per record found

WESTERN LIBRARY NETWORK

MICRO RECON

Hardware	IBM PC or Apple II
Software	WLN provided; prompts user for LCCN and WLN RID, then to enter local data
Database	LCMARC (Books, Serials, Music, etc.), CANMARC; LCMARC and CANMARC authorities
Access	LCCN; WLN RID obtained from COM Resource Directory or CD-ROM version of WLN database; title
Products and reports	Fiche; magnetic tape; catalog cards and labels; hard copy catalogs; CD-ROM catalogs
Costs	Software: $75 $.30/hit

Online via dial-up

Hardware	Dial-up via most micros
Software	Dial-up via common communications programs
Database	The online system currently offers 4.7 million records under authority control
Access	Title, author, subject, series and Boolean search strategies
Products and reports	Fiche; magnetic tape; catalog cards and labels; hard copy catalogs; CD-ROM catalogs
Costs	Upon request

LaserCat

Hardware	Via tested IBM compatibles including the model 30; 2 CD-ROM drives, either Hitachi or Sony
Database	Contains all records with holdings, and current LC cataloging for the past two years without holdings, about 2.4 million records
Access	Author, title, subject, ISBN, LCCN, ISSN; exact or keyword author, title, subject; truncation; browsing
Software	LaserCat software including cards and labels program
Products and reports	Fiche; magnetic tape; catalog cards and labels; hard copy catalogs; CD-ROM catalogs
Costs	$1,300 per year for four issues

WLN Catalog and Input Service

Hardware	None
Software	None
Database	Complete WLN database
Access	Title, author, series, subjects, ISBN, LCCN, ISSN
Products and reports	Fiche; magnetic tape; catalog cards and labels; hard copy catalogs; CD-ROM catalogs
Costs	Upon request

Appendix II
Directory of Recon Vendors

Amigos Bibliographic Council, Inc.
11300 North Central Expressway,
Suite 321
Dallas, TX 75243
(800) 843-8482 (USA only)

Auto-Graphics, Inc.
3201 Temple Ave.
Pomona, CA 91768
(800) 325-7961 (USA only)
(800) 828-9585 (California)
(714) 595-7204

Blackwell North America
6024 S.W. Jean Rd.
Building G
Lake Oswego, OR 97035
(800) 547-6426 (USA)
(800) 626-1807 (Canada)
(503) 684-1140

Brodart Automation
500 Arch St.
Williamsport, PA 17705-9977
(800) 233-8467 (Eastern USA)
(800) 643-0523 (Western USA)
(800) 821-1117 (California)
(717) 326-2461

The Computer Company
P.O. Box 6987
1905 Westmoreland St.
Richmond, VA 23230
(800) 327-5160 (USA only)
(804) 254-2200

EKI Inc.
140 Weldon Pkwy.
St. Louis, MO 63043-3180
(800) 325-4984 (USA only)
(314) 567-1780

Gaylord Information Systems
20251 Century Blvd.
Germantown, MD 20874-1162
(800) 638-8725 (USA only)
(301) 428-3400

General Research Corporation
5383 Hollister Ave.
P.O. Box 6770
Santa Barbara, CA 93160-6770
(800) 235-6788
(805) 964-7724

Information Transform Inc.
502 Leonard St.
Madison, WI 53711
(608) 255-4800

The Library Corporation
P.O. Box 40035
Washington, DC 20016
(800) 624-0559 (USA only)
(304) 725-7220

Library of Congress
Processing Services
Cataloging Distribution Service
Washington, DC 20541
(202) 287-1308

Library Technologies, Inc.,
1142E Bradfield Road,
Abington, PA 19001
(215) 576-6983

Marcive, Inc.
P.O. Box 47508
San Antonio, TX 78265-7508
(800) 531-7678 (USA only)
(512) 646-6161

National Library of Canada
Canadiana Editorial Division
395 Wellington St.
Ottawa, Ontario K1A 0N4
Canada
(819) 994-6913

OCLC
6565 Frantz Rd.
Dublin, OH 43017-0702
(800) 848-5878 (USA)
(800) 533-8201 (Canada)
(614) 764-6000

Ontario Library Services Center
141 Dearborn Place
Waterloo, Ontario
Canada
N2J 4N5
(519) 746-4420

Retro Link Associates, Ltd.,
175 North Freedom Boulevard, Suite 202,
Provo, UT 84601
(801) 375-6508

RLIN
Research Libraries Group
Jordan Quadrangle
Stanford, CA 94305
(415) 328-0920

SAZTEC International
975 Oak St., Suite 615
Eugene, OR 97401
(503) 343-8640

SOLINET
Southern Library Network, Inc.
Plaza Level, 400 Colony Square
1201 Peachtree Street, N.E.
Atlanta, GA 30361
(404) 892-0943

Utlas International Canada
80 Bloor St. West, 2nd. Floor,
Toronto, Ontario M5S 2V1
Canada
M5S 2V1
(416) 923-0890

Utlas International U.S. Inc.,
8300 College Blvd.
Overland Park, KS 66210
(800) 338-8527

Western Library Network
Washington State Library, AJ-11W
Olympia, WA 98504-0111
(206) 459-6518

Appendix III
Sample Forms for the Preparation of Bibliographic Records

Most libraries find it useful to have a worksheet for current cataloging. It may not be necessary to use it for every record created in the online system, but it is useful for training new catalogers, and original catalogers who have to gather information from a number of sources may find it useful in preparation for entering the completed record. The following worksheets are provided as examples from two of our client libraries: the Leddy Library, University of Windsor and King's College, London, Ontario. Using these forms as a basis we suggest you create a form that suits your needs and requirements.

CURRENT CATALOGUING WORKSHEET

1. Level of processing:
2. ISBD Status:
3. LC card no:
4. ISBN:
5. Edition statement:
6. Publication date:
7. Publisher:
8. Publishing country:
9. Languages:
10. Author(s):

11. Uniform title:

12. Title:

    Number of characters to skip:

13. Physical features:

14. Series:

15. Notes

16. Local characteristics:
17. LC Call number:
18. Keywords:
19. Subject headings:

20. Item information:
    1. Usual location   2. Shelving number
    3. Volume   4. Circ. category
    5. Inventory status   6. Notes
    7. Temp. location   8. Temp. circ. category
    9. Reserve room

RECORD NUMBER:

MARC CODING SHEET: Monographs   RECORD ID:

Fixed: Type date: _   Date1: ____   Date2: ____   Country: ___
                Int.level: _   Form. repr: _ Fiction: _   Language: ___

Variable fields:

TAG	IND 1	2	

MARC CODING SHEET: Monographs   **RECORD ID:**

Type date: _   Date1: ____   Date2: ____   Country: ___
Int.level: _   Form. repr: _   Fiction: _   Language: ___

Variable fields:

TAG	IND 1	2	
010			
020			
1__			
245			
250			
260			
300			
4__			
5__			
6__			
7__			
8__			

Initials: Date:

Appendix IV
Selected Bibliography

Retrospective Conversion

Adler, A.G., and E.A. Baber, eds. *Retrospective Conversion: From Cards to Computer*. Ann Arbor, MI: Pieran Press, 1984.

Asher, Richard E. "Retrospective Conversion of Bibliographic Records." *Catholic Library World* 54 (November 1982): 155-61.

Auld, Lawrence W. S. "Retrospective Catalog Conversion Costs." Chap. 15 in *Electronic Spreadsheets for Libraries*. Phoenix, AZ: Oryx Press, 1986.

Avram, Henriette D. "Toward a Nationwide Library Network." *Journal of Library Administration* 8 (Fall-Winter 1987): 95-116.

Awcock, Frances. "Retrospective Conversion: Pipedream or Practicality?" *Australian Library Journal* 34 (February 1985): 11-18.

Baldwin, Paul E., and Leigh Swain. *RECON Alternatives for Eight British Columbia Public Libraries: An Ancillary Report for the British Columbia Library Network Prepared at the Request of the Greater Vancouver Library Federation and Greater Victoria Public Library*. Richmond, BC: British Columbia Union Catalogue, 1980.

Banach, Patricia, and Cynthia Spell. "Serials Conversion at the University of Massachusetts at Amherst." *Information Technology and Libraries* 7 (June 1988): 124-30.

Beaumont, Jane. "Retrospective Conversion on a Micro: Options for Libraries." *Library Software Review* 5 (July-August 1986): 213-18.

Bocher, Robert. "MITINET: Catalog Conversion to a MARC Database." *School Library Journal* 31 (March 1985): 109-12.

Boss, Richard W. *Issues in Retrospective Conversion*. N.p.: R.W. Boss, 1985.

———. "Retrospective Conversion: Investing in the Future." *Wilson Library Bulletin* 59 (November 1984): 173-78.

———, and Hal Espo. "Standards, Database Design, & Retrospective Conversion." *Library Journal* 112 (October 1, 1987): 54-58.

Burger, Robert H. "Conversion of Catalog Records to Machine-Readable Form: Major Projects, Continuing Problems, and Future Prospects." *Cataloging & Classification Quarterly* 3 (Fall 1982): 27-40.

Butler, Brett, Brian Aveney, and William Scholz. "The Conversion of Manual Catalogs to Collection Data Bases." *Library Technology Reports* 14 (March-April 1978): 109-206.

Carter, Ruth C., and Scott Bruntjen. *Data Conversion*. Professional Librarian Series. White Plains, NY: Knowledge Industry Publications, 1983.

Chiang, Belinda. *Retrospective Conversion through Carrollton Press: Manual of Procedures for Colgate University Libraries*. N.p.: Colgate University Library, 1983.

Cobb, David A. "Online Bibliographic and Circulation Systems: The Illinois Example." *INSPEL* 22, no. 1 (1988): 48-55.

Collins, Jane D. "Planning for Retrospective Conversion." *Art Documentation* 1 (Summer 1982): 92-94.

Copeland, Nora S. "Retrospective Conversion of Serials: The RLIN Experience." *Serials Review* 14 (Fall 1988): 23-28.

Crismond, Linda F. "Quality Issues in Retrospective Conversion Projects." *Library Resources & Technical Services* 25 (January-March 1981): 48-55.

Desmarais, Norman. "BiblioFile for Retrospective Conversion." *Small Computers in Libraries* 5 (December 1985): 24-28.

DiCarlo, Michael A. "Sequential Analysis as a Sampling Test for Accuracy of Retrospective Conversion." In *Conference on Integrated Online Library Systems, September 23 and 24, 1986, St. Louis, Missouri: Proceedings*, compiled and edited by David C. Genaway. Canfield, OH: Genaway & Associates, 1987.

————, and Margaret W. Maxfield. "Sequential Analysis as a Sampling Test for Inventory Need." *The Journal of Academic Librarianship* 13 (January 1988): 345-48.

Douglas, Nancy E. "REMARC Retrospective Conversion: What, Why, and How." *Technical Services Quarterly* 2 (Spring-Summer 1985): 11-16.

Drabenstott, Jon, ed. "Retrospective Conversion: Issues and Perspectives: A Forum." *Library Hi Tech* 4 (Summer 1986): 105-20.

Dwyer, James R. "The Effect of Closed Catalogs on Public Access." *Library Resources & Technical Services* 25 (April-June 1981): 186-95.

Epstein, Hank. "MITINET/retro: Retrospective Conversion on an Apple." *Information Technology and Libraries* 2 (June 1983): 166-73.

————. "A System for Retrospective Conversion." *American Libraries* 15 (February 1984): 113-14.

Epstein, Susan Baerg. "Converting Bibliographic Records for Automation: Some Options." *Library Journal* 108 (March 1, 1983): 474-76.

————. "Converting Records for Automation at the Copy Level." *Library Journal* 108 (April 1, 1983): 642-43.

Ferrell, Mary Sue, and Carol A. Parkhurst. "Using LaserQuest for Retrospective Conversion of MARC Records." *Optical Information Systems* 7 (November-December 1987): 396-400.

Garland, Catherine. "PREMARC: Retrospective Conversion at the Library of Congress." *Fontes Artis Musicae* 34 (April-September 1987): 132-38.

Gartshore, Tom. "BiblioFile and the School Library." *School Libraries in Canada* 7 (Winter 1987): 36-40.

Gorman, Michael. "The Economics of Catalog Conversion." In *Proceedings of the 1976 Clinic on Library Applications of Data Processing: The Economics of Library Automation*, edited by J.L. Divilbiss. Champaign, Ill.: University of Illinois, Graduate School of Library Science, 1977.

Gregor, Dorothy, comp. and ed. *Retrospective Conversion of Music Materials: Report of a Meeting Sponsored by the Council on Library Resources, July 18-19, 1984, Wayzata, Minnesota*. Washington, D.C.: Bibliographic Service Development Program, Council on Library Resources, 1984.

_____. *Retrospective Conversion: Report of a Meeting Sponsored by the Council on Library Resources, July 16-18, 1984, Wayzata, Minnesota*. Washington, D.C.: Bibliographic Service Development Program, Council on Library Resources, 1984.

"Guidelines Proposed for Retrospective Conversion of Bibliographic Records of Monographs." *Library of Congress Information Bulletin* 44 (March 25, 1985): 59-60.

Harrison, Martin. "Retrospective Conversion of Card Catalogues into Full MARC Format Using Sophisticated Computer-Controlled Visual Imaging Techniques." *Program* 19 (July 1985): 213-30.

Hein, Morten. "Optical Scanning for Retrospective Conversion of Information." *Electronic Library* 4 (December 1986): 328-31.

Heitshu, Sara C., and Joan M. Quinn. "Serials Conversion at the University of Michigan." *Drexel Library Quarterly* 21 (Winter 1985): 62-76.

Hirshon, Arnold. "The Emperor's Bibliographic Clothes." *RTSD Newsletter* 10, no. 3 (1985): 28-30.

Hoadley, Irene B., and Leila Payne. "Toward Tomorrow: A Retrospective Conversion Project." *Journal of Academic Librarianship* 9 (July 1983): 138-41.

Hoare, Peter A. "Retrospective Catalogue Conversion in British University Libraries: A Survey and a Discussion of Problems." *British Journal of Academic Librarianship* 1 (Summer 1986): 95-131.

Information Systems Consultants Inc. *Automation Options for the Regional Libraries of Alberta: Final Report*. N.p.: Information Systems Consultants Inc., 1984.

_____. *Retrospective Conversion for the Libraries of McGill University*. N.p.: Information Systems Consultants Inc., 1984.

"Instant MARC at Cornwall County Library." *Vine* 24 (August 1978): 17-19.

Intner, Sheila S. "Bibliographic Policies." *Technicalities* 7 (August 1987): 3-6.

Johnson, Carolyn A. "Retrospective Conversion of Three Library Collections." *Information Technology and Libraries* 1 (June 1982): 133-39.

Jones, C. Lee. "Issues in Retrospective Conversion." *College and Research Libraries News* 45 (November 1984): 528-32.

Juneja, Derry C. "Quality Control in Data Conversion." *Library Resources & Technical Services* 31 (April-June 1987): 148-58.

Kaplan, Denise P. "Creating Copy Specific Records for Local Databases." *Library Hi Tech* 2, no. 3 (1984): 19-24.

Kawamoto, Chizuko. "File Analysis for Retrospective Conversion: The Case of the California State Library, Law Library." *Law Library Journal* 79 (Summer 1987): 455-67.

Kruger, Kathleen Joyce. "MARC Tags and Retrospective Conversion: The Editing Process." *Information Technology and Libraries* 4 (March 1985): 53-57.

Law, Derek. "The State of Retroconversion in the United Kingdom: A Review." *Journal of Librarianship* 20 (April 1988): 81-93.

Lisowski, Andrew. "Vendor-Based Retrospective Conversion at George Washington University." *Library Hi Tech* 1 (Winter 1983): 23-26.

———, and Judith Sessions. "Selecting a Retrospective Conversion Vendor." *Library Hi Tech* 1 (Spring 1984): 65-68.

"Loading Separate Bibliographic Files on an Automated System." *Library Systems Newsletter* 4 (September 1984): 69-71.

"Machine-Readable Cataloging Data Providers." *Library Systems Newsletter* 5 (November 1985): 86-88.

MacMillan, Gary D. "UTLAS DISCON: REMARC/MARC on CD-ROM in Hawaii." *CD-ROM Librarian* 2 (September-October 1987): 12-15.

Martin, Norma H. "Non-MARC and MLC Records: To Upgrade or Not?" *RTSD Newsletter* 13 (Winter 1987): 1-3.

Matthews, Joseph R., and Joan Frye Williams. "Oh, If I'd Only Known: Ten Things You Can Do Today to Prepare for Library Automation Tomorrow." *American Libraries* 14 (June 1983): 408-12.

McGill University. Libraries/Systems Office. *Summary of a New Method for RECON.* Montreal: The Office, 1985.

McQueen, Judy, and Richard W. Boss. "Sources of Machine-Readable Cataloging and Retrospective Conversion." *Library Technology Reports* 21 (November-December 1985): 601-732.

Merrett, C., and Colleen Vietzen. "Aspects of Card Catalogue Conversion at the University of Natal Library, Pietermaritzburg." *South African Journal of Library and Information Science* 53 (June 1985): 89-94.

Miller, Bruce Cummings. "Spreadsheet Models of Library Activities." *Library Hi Tech* 1 (Spring 1984): 19-25.

Millican, Rita. "Serials Conversion: LSU's Experience." *Serials Librarian* 9 (Summer 1985): 45-51.

"OCLC, AMIGOS and SOLINET Retrospective Conversion." *Library Hi Tech News* no. 13 (February 1985): 5-6.

"OCR-Based Retrospective Conversion." *Library Systems Newsletter* 5 (January 1985): 1-2.

Olsen, Vivian. "Three Research Libraries Convert Music Materials." *Research Libraries in OCLC* 23 (Summer 1987): 1-7.

"'Ownership' of Machine-Readable Records: A Neglected Consideration in Retrospective Conversion." *Library Systems Newsletter* 4 (June 1984): 43-46.

Peters, Stephen H., and Douglas J. Butler. "A Cost Model for Retrospective Conversion Alternatives." *Library Resources & Technical Services* 28 (April-June 1984): 149-51, 154-62.

Petersen, Karla D. "Planning for Serials Retrospective Conversion." *Serials Review* 10 (Fall 1984): 73-78.

Purnell, Kathleen M. "Productivity in a Large-Scale Retrospective Conversion Project." In *Productivity in the Information Age: Proceedings of the 46th ASIS Annual Meeting 1983*, edited by Raymond F. Vondran, Anne Caputo, Carol Wasserman, and Richard A.V. Diener. White Plains, NY: Knowledge Industry Publications for American Society for Information Science, 1983.

Ra, Marsha. "The Need for Costing in a Cooperative Retrospective Conversion Project." *Technical Services Quarterly* 4 (Summer 1987): 39-48.

Racine, Drew. "Retrospective Conversion: A Challenge (Still) Facing Academic Libraries." *Show-Me Libraries* 36 (October-November 1984): 39-43.

Raitt, David. "CD-ROM Review: LaserQuest." *The Electronic Library* 6 (June 1988): 198-202.

Rearden, Phyllis, and John A. Whisler. "Retrospective Conversion at Eastern Illinois University." *Illinois Libraries* 65 (May 1983): 343-46.

"RECON and REMARC and Edinburgh University Library." *Vine* no. 49 (August 1983): 13-18.

Reed-Scott, Jutta. *Plan for a North American Program for Coordinated Retrospective Conversion.* Washington, DC: Association of Research Libraries, 1985.

————. "Retrospective Conversion: An Update." *American Libraries* 16 (November 1985): 694, 696, 698.

————, Dorothy Gregor, and Charles Payne. *Issues in Retrospective Conversion: Report of a Study Conducted for the Council on Library Resources.* Washington, DC: Council on Library Resources, 1984.

"Retrospective Conversion." *Information Technology and Libraries* 3 (September 1984): 267-78, 280-84, 286-92.

Retrospective Conversion. SPEC Kit, no. 130. Washington, DC: Office of Management Studies, Association of Research Libraries, 1987.

Richardson, Valerie. "Retrospective Conversion Using LYNX and REMARC." *LASIE* 14 (September-October 1983): 14-25.

Ricker, Karina. "A Geac Library's Experience with Microcon." *RTSD Newsletter* 12 (Fall 1987): 44-46.

Rogers, Gloria H. "From Cards to Online: The Asian Connection." *Information Technology and Libraries* 5 (December 1986): 280-84.

Ross, John, and Bruce Royan. "Backfile Conversion Today: CIM Era or Chimera?" *Program* 11 (October 1977): 156-65.

Ryans, Cynthia C. "Retrospective Conversion to a Machine-Readable System." *Technicalities* 1 (August 1981): 5-6, 12.

————, and Margaret F. Soule. "Preparations for Retrospective Conversion: An Empirical Study." *Catholic Library World* 55 (December 1983): 221-23.

Severtson, Susan. "REMARC: A Retrospective Conversion Project." *Program* 17 (October 1983): 224-32.

Smith, Sharon, Robert Watkins, and Shirley Richardson. "Retrospective Conversion of Serials at the University of Houston: Midterm Report." *Serials Librarian* 9 (Spring 1985): 63-68.

Valentine, Phyllis A., and David R. McDonald. "Retrospective Conversion: A Question of Time, Standards, and Purpose." *Information Technology and Libraries* 5 (June 1986): 112-20.

Watkins, Deane. "Record Conversion at Oregon State." *Wilson Library Bulletin* 60 (December 1985): 31-33.

Wells, Kathleen L. "Retrospective Conversion: Through the Looking Glass." *RTSD Newsletter* 12 (Winter 1987): 10-11.

Wood, Susan. *Retrospective Conversion Procedure Manual for the Health Sciences Library.* Chapel Hill, NC: Health Sciences Library, University of North Carolina at Chapel Hill, 1984.

MARC

American National Standards Institute. *American National Standard for Bibliographic Information Interchange on Magnetic Tape.* New York: ANSI, 1979.

Attig, John C. "The Concept of a MARC Format." *Information Technology and Libraries* 2 (March 1983): 7-17.

―――. "US/MARC Formats: Underlying Principles." *Library of Congress Information Bulletin* 41 (April 23, 1982): 120-24.

Bills, Linda G., and Linda W. Helgerson. "CD-ROM Public Access Catalogs: Database Creation and Maintenance." *Library Hi Tech* 6, no 1 (1988) : 67-86.

Bowerman, Roseann, and Susan Anne Cady. "Government Publications in an Online Catalog: A Feasibility Study." *Information Technology and Libraries* 3 (December 1984): 331-42.

British Standards Institution. *Bibliographic Information Interchange Format for Magnetic Tape.* London: BSI, 1971.

Byrne, Deborah. "The Much-Misunderstood MARC Fixed Field." *Action for Libraries* 13 (February 1987): 4; 13 (March 1987): 4-5.

Chatterton, Leigh. "Exploring the US MARC Format For Holdings and Locations: Should We Consider It for Our Records?" *The Serials Librarian* 13 (October-November 1987): 143-45.

City of London Polytechnic Library. "Machine-Readable Cataloguing Data Providers." *Library Systems Newsletter* 5 (November 1985): 86-88.

Crawford, W. *MARC for Library Use: Understanding the USMARC Formats.* White Plains, NY: Knowledge Industry Publications, 1984.

Dalehite, Michele I. "MARC Format on Tape: A Tutorial." *Library Hi Tech* 2 (1984): 17-21.

Epstein, Hank. "An Expert System for Novice MARC Catalogers." *Wilson Library Bulletin* 62 (November 87): 33-36.

―――. "The First Step in Ohio School Library/Media Automation: A Leadership Challenge (Using MITINET)." *Ohio Media Spectrum* 40 (Spring 1988): 14-24.

Garcia, Florencio Oscar, and Ursula Noher. *Librarian's Puzzle: MARC, CIP, ISBN, OCLC, RLIN.* N.p.: FOG Publications, 1988.

Harrison, Martin. "Retrospective Conversion of Card Catalogues into Full MARC Format Using Sophisticated Computer-Controlled Visual Imaging Techniques." *Program* 19 (July 1985): 213-30.

Honhart, Frederick L. "The Application of Microcomputer-Based Local Systems with the MARC AMC Format." *Library Trends* 36 (Winter 1988): 585-92.

Kruger, Kathleen Joyce. "MARC Tags and Retrospective Conversion: The Editing Process." *Information Technology and Libraries* 4 (March 1985): 53-57.

Library of Congress. Automated Systems Office. *MARC Formats for Bibliographic Data.* Washington, DC: Library of Congress, 1980- . Looseleaf.

———. Automation Planning and Liaison Office. *Authorities: A MARC Format.* Washington, DC: Library of Congress, 1981.

———. Network Development and MARC Standards Office. *USMARC Authority Format Including Guidelines for Content Designation.* Washington, DC: Library of Congress, 1987- . Looseleaf. (Superintendent of Documents No. LC1.6/4:Au8)

———. *USMARC Specifications for Record Structure, Character Sets, Tapes.* Washington, DC: Library of Congress, 1987.

———. Subject Cataloging Division. Processing Services. *Library of Congress Subject Headings.* 11th Edition. Washington, DC: Library of Congress, 1988.

Litchfield, Charles A., and Marilyn L. "Coded Holdings: A Primer for New Users." *Serials Review* 14, no. 1-2 (1988): 81-88.

Matthews, Joseph R., and Joan Frye Williams. "Oh, If I'd Only Known: Ten Things You Can Do Today to Prepare for Library Automation Tomorrow." *American Libraries* 14 (June 1983): 418-12.

McDonald, David R. "MARC: the Foundation of Library Automation." *Journal of Academic Librarianship* 13 (July 1987): 168c-168d : insert between 168-69.

National Library of Canada. *Canadian MARC Communication Format: Minimal Level.* Ottawa: National Library of Canada, 1987.

———. *Canadian MARC Communication Format: Mini-MARC.* Ottawa: National Library of Canada, 1982.

———. *Canadian Subject Headings.* 2d. Edition. Ottawa: 1985. (DSS cat. no. SN3-106/1985)

———. Canadian MARC Office. *Canadian MARC Communications Format: Bibliographic Data.* Ottawa: National Library of Canada, 1988- . Looseleaf. (DSS cat. no. SN214/1988E)

———. *Canadian MARC Communications Format: Authorities.* 3rd. Edition. Ottawa: National Library of Canada, 1988- . Looseleaf. (DSS cat. no. SN3-123/1988E)

Raithel, Frederick J.   "READMARC: A Simple BASIC Program to Read MARC Bibliographic Records." *Small Computers in Libraries* 7 (April 1987): 33-35.

Reynolds, Jon K. "MicroMARC:amc." *American Archivist* 50(Spring 1987): 266-68.

Simmons, Peter, and Alan Hopkinson. *CCF: The Common Communications Format.* Paris: Unesco For The General Information Programme and UNISIST, 1984.

Smith, Robert.   "MARC Record Supply: the British Library Reacts to a Changing Environment." *Library Association Record* 89 (September 1987): 466.

Visk, Linda Sapp. "The USMARC Format for Holdings and Locations." *Drexel Library Quarterly* 21 (Winter 1985): 87-100.

Wiggins, Beacher.   "The Processing and Distribution of International MARC Data by the Library of Congress." *International Leads* 2 (Spring 1988): 7.

Zboray, Ronald J.   "dBase III Plus and the MARC AMC Format: Problems and Possibilities." *American Archivist* 50 (Spring 1987): 210-25.

Index

About the Authors

Jane Beaumont is a library and information systems consultant based in Toronto, Canada.

Joseph P. Cox is Catalog Librarian, Faculty of Library and Information Science Library, University of Toronto.